CONVERSATIONS WITH
HARRIET BULLITT

CONVERSATIONS WITH HARRIET BULLITT

The Development of Sleeping Lady Mountain Retreat

WERNER JANSSEN

ISBN: 9798673270950

We have three icons in the State of Washington:

One is Mount Rainier,

The second is the Columbia River,

The third is Harriet Bullitt,

All larger than life.

—Washington State Governor Jay Inslee at Harriet's birthday party
and the unveiling of the Snowy Owl Theater in 2013
Reported by Joel Connelly, Seattle PI, September 16, 2013

CONTENTS

Foreword

⚬⚬⚬

IT IS A GREAT HONOR to be invited by my friend Werner Janssen to write the foreword for *Conversations with Harriet Bullitt*. Her impact on North Central Washington over the last quarter century has been nothing short of transformative, yet for many people, Harriet has been an enigma.

Janssen is uniquely qualified to share with us his insights and perspective on Harriet's philanthropic work in this region. He was the manager of Holden Village for many years and was hired by Harriet as her first manager at Sleeping Lady Mountain Retreat. Not only did he have a bird's-eye view of how she went about making a difference as a colleague, he also recorded numerous conversations that probed into her thinking and values. The insights he has been able to tease out give this narrative a rich texture that is often missed in similar efforts.

Conversations with Harriet is a story that needed to be written and deserves to be read and remembered, to inspire all of us to use our influence and resources to make our communities better places. Janssen, who is self-publishing the book, has given us a great gift.

Harriet grew up in a family of privilege in the exclusive Seattle Highlands and went on to be involved in the broadcasting empire at KING. In her seventies she turned her attention to creating something meaningful and transformative in North Central Washington by creating Sleeping Lady Mountain Retreat and launching the Icicle Fund to support environmental projects, education, history, and the arts. The Icicle Fund has invested more than $30 million in the region in support of these causes and provides ongoing support for five key nonprofits—Icicle Creek Center for the Arts, the Chelan-Douglas Land Trust, the Methow Arts Alliance, The Nature Conservancy, and The Trust for Public Land.

She stands with great philanthropists like Warren Buffett and Bill Gates, who have chosen to use their tremendous resources to support the greater good rather than hording wealth for themselves. "To whom much is given, much will be required," Luke 12:48(NRSV) reminds us. Harriet Bullitt exemplified that philanthropic mindset.

One aspect of Harriet's approach that has impressed me is that she makes contributions quietly. You won't find Harriet Bullitt's name on any buildings in North Central Washington, but you can clearly see what she values by what she supports.

In *Conversations with Harriet Bullitt*, Janssen gives us an inside look at her motivations and her unique way of getting things done. With Harriet, what you see is authentic. She doesn't put on a separate public persona. Like a Möbius strip, her internal values are accurately reflected in her external actions. This book invites us to follow her example of living an authentic life and using one's gifts and talents in our sphere of influence to make our community and our country a better place.

—Rufus Woods, Publisher Emeritus
The Wenatchee World

A Tribute

How DO I WRITE A tribute to a person as storied as Harriet Bullitt? How do I adequately describe Harriet's deep spirit, wisdom, and wit? When I see Harriet, I see color.

Harriet was seventy-five when we met. She and Werner interviewed me for a Human Resource position at Sleeping Lady Retreat Center. After a conversation about this position, Harriet asked, "How would you like to be my personal assistant?" We both laughed about this suggestion, and I told her "I've never been an assistant; I can barely take care of myself." Harriet said, "That's OK. My other assistants didn't like working for me because I'd forget where I was supposed to be, and that was frustrating to them." We agreed to give this relationship a trial run. I would point her in the right direction at the right time, and I promised not to get frustrated if she didn't get there. Twenty years later we are still together. My relationship with Harriet has transformed over the years, established as employer, moving to mentor, flourishing into friendship, and maturing into deep love, agape love. You just cannot plan a career like this.

Harriet was a patient mentor. We would sort through stacks of mail as I tried to understand what was important to her, what needed to be saved for future reference, and what could be discarded. It became clear early on: keep all the equestrian magazines and the flamenco dance newsletters. Business mail was left to my discretion.

Harriet shared her wisdom with me often. One day we were in the office when she received a phone call that a close friend had died. When the call ended, Harriet said to me, "Be sure you make new friends all your life. Make friends with people much younger than you, not just your own age. Then if you live a long life, you'll never outlive your friends." Harriet is currently ninety-six years old. She is still richly blessed with friends.

People who know Harriet know that she has a quick wit. One morning on her way to saddling her horse for a daily ride, dressed in her blue jeans and riding boots, I told her a man had called and asked to meet with her to discuss a business opportunity that would make her a lot of money. Harriet said, "I already have a lot of money. I'm going to ride my horse."

Harriet has always been an active person who does not like spending time indoors. We would both agree on the time to meet to review business matters, but the location was up to Harriet. She seldom chose the office. Harriet avoided the office and could sneak out right from under my eyes. She was like Houdini when she wanted to make an exit. Or she would wait until I was on the phone and slip past my desk, blue eyes sparkling, making the sign gesture for walking away. Poof! Gone before I could ask where I could find her later.

In the early days, Harriet was either on her bike or on her skis. It's not too difficult to talk business while riding a bike; skis were more difficult. Then came the horses. When you are not an equestrian, it's much harder to discuss business while bouncing on the back of a horse. The logistics are complicated: Where do I keep my notebook? How do I hold my coffee mug, my notebook, and the reins? I soon realized that these "meetings" were less about business and more about teaching me to ride. Rather than give me an answer for an email that needed a response, Harriet would remind me to keep my toes up and heels down in the stirrups. Confirming a date and time on her calendar for a business call became the date and time on her calendar for the next equestrian drill team practice. Never knowing where my workday would be located, I kept a pair of shoes in my office that were stirrup approved. I would escape these lessons by telling Harriet that I needed to get back to the office before my boss finds out I'm out riding horses.

The magic of Harriet is her wit and fun-loving nature. However, Harriet is also publicly known for her deep commitment to the environment and to the arts as well as her philanthropic gifts. Harriet has provided many such gifts in her lifetime, but ensuring music and art education is available to every child is one of Harriet's core values.

However, through the years our close relationship has allowed me the view to see that Harriet's deepest commitment is to her family. From the very beginning, Harriet instructed me to only accept meeting requests from those who understood that she might cancel at the last minute if her family was visiting.

Harriet loved it when her family showed up at Coppernotch for a weekend or a month. She considered this time with her children and grandchildren priceless. These family visits were protected from business distractions at all costs, even if it meant cancelling a meeting planned for weeks.

Time and time again, someone would request a meeting with Harriet to discuss various topics or request funding for projects. More than once Harriet would call me in the morning to tell me about an unexpected family visit. She would ask me to please call whoever was arriving that morning for a meeting to let them know she was not available. Most were understanding. The people and organizations who knew Harriet the best, and had the sincerest relationships with her, were always gracious.

Today Harriet continues to teach me the value in finding something to care deeply about, and to give it the full attention it deserves. She has demonstrated this through her relationships with her family, friends, and her community.

Maybe it is no wonder that I see Harriet as color. I see her blue swim-suit as she swims in Icicle Creek. I see red in all the things she loves. I see bright white bursts of light and energy that shine onto a beautiful picture of a beautiful soul.

With agape love to you, Harriet,
Deborah Hartl, assistant to Harriet Bullitt

Introduction

———⚬⚬⚬———

WRITING A BOOK COVERING THE life of Harriet Bullitt is a delightful challenge. Harriet is an amazing person who has remained honest to herself and her convictions throughout her life. Harriet has, in the process, enriched so many lives, while giving a powerful, loving hug to nature. I want to clarify what I have written is not a history of Harriet's life. Her life is far too expansive and even complicated for my limited research ability. These conversations resulted from my questions and her impromptu thoughts and did not specifically cover all aspects of her life. A good portion of the first six chapters are direct transcripts of the recorded conversations.

I worked with Harriet developing the Sleeping Lady Mountain Retreat. Harriet also gave me the opportunity to serve as the general manager of the operation for a time. During those years we enjoyed many hours of conversations on topics not always related to the Sleeping Lady project. Harriet was very open with me about many aspects of her life and also permitted me to record conversations after I approached her about writing a book about her. Many of our early conversation occurred at Sleeping Lady's O'Grady's Pantry and Grotto Bar or at her chalet over a meal. It was a delight to visit with her on her beautiful tug, the *Owl*, moored in the ship canal. I had the privilege of doing a Story Corp interview with Harriet in June of 2009, lending additional insights. She provided several editorials, broadcast on her radio station, KOHO 101.1 FM, sharing interesting thoughts and personal memories. In the last several years, I have recorded many hours of conversations with Harriet covering a wide range of topics. The most recent conversation occurred at her new home on the hillside above the Chihuly sculpture along the banks of her beloved Icicle Creek. My conversations and recordings occurred up to September 2018. I visited with Harriet for a couple of hours in June 2019 but did not record or take notes of that conversation. It was a conversation of friendship and gratitude.

It became clear to me that a historical writing of Harriet's life would be beyond my capabilities but sharing some of her life through our conversations would be feasible. What I write is partly a memoir of a portion of Harriet's life and partly my time working with Harriet for over ten years. Serving on the three-person development team during the construction phase was a significant part of my time becoming well acquainted with Harriet. I also served as a board member of the Sleeping Lady Foundation and the Icicle Creek Music Center. Harriet also invited me to broadcast commentaries weekly on KOHO 101.1 FM over numerous years. The development of Sleeping Lady Mountain Retreat helps illustrate how her life and her convictions were deeply entwined with the conceptual ideas she had in developing not only the facility but also the operational philosophy.

Harriet's life has been dedicated to following her convictions developed while growing up in a rather powerful family but never abusing her wealth or power to realize her desires and dreams.

Education did not come easily for Harriet, but wisdom, perseverance, and financial means provided the possibilities to continue her life's journey, resulting in many great accomplishments. Harriet was guided in her life through the influence of her grandparents and parents, in terms of both observed influences and powerful genes. Great family DNA flowed through several generations, making it possible for her to learn through observed opportunities, always finding ways to accomplish what convictions inspired.

Harriet never hesitated to acknowledge that she grew up in a family of privilege. Money and influence, when used for the good of humanity and nature, is a gift, and she used these gifts to help and benefit others. She is a humble person with powerful influence and a feisty side when she is challenged by ideas or concepts she questions.

Harriet was privileged to grow up at a time when freedom to explore both thought and nature was encouraged. She made good use exploring both. She always valued friendships and has lived an exciting life utilizing the benefits provided through friendships and acquaintances, rather than through a master plan developed by family or professional direction.

Harriet began her life in the exclusive Seattle Highlands. In her seventies she moved to where her heart was always the happiest, the family property along the Icicle Creek outside of Leavenworth, Washington.

The impact Harriet has had on so many lives as well as the nature she loves culminated in her development of Sleeping Lady Mountain Retreat and the Icicle Creek Music Center. Her passion for life, her persistence bringing into reality what she learned through her family ties, and the expression of her strong convictions resulted in the miracle of these developments. Numerous other organizations were created through her initiative, positively enhancing life in the Northwest through her philanthropy and unending energy.

What I share will encompass her early life growing up with strong family connections, her struggle with formal education, her love for art, music, and nature, and her honesty and determination to follow her convictions. This is far from a complete history of Harriet's life.

Perhaps the most powerful force that Harriet displayed through the years is her generosity inviting others to explore their dreams while helping her fulfill her own dreams. What I have written is based on my time working directly with Harriet as an employee from 1993 through 2003 and our continued friendship.

I write this as one who greatly admires Harriet as a friend and one who has been privileged to work with her.

Thank you, Harriet.

—Werner Janssen, 2020   chbwcj@gmail.com

CHAPTER 1
In the Beginning

———∞∞∞———

OPENING EDITORIAL WRITTEN BY HARRIET Bullitt—KOHO 101.1 FM broadcast, Christmas Day, 2012

A long time ago, a little girl, with a boy cousin her age, an older sister, mother, and grandmother board a Great North-ern train at King Street station, bound for Leavenworth, Washington. Christmas vacation promises fun in the snow.

Gray scenery passes the train windows. Stop and go. Let people on and off...exchange mail in Everett, Monroe, Sul-tan, Startup, Goldbar, Index, Baring, Scenic. This stop is for engineers to take off the coal-fired engine, park it, and latch on the new electric one. The train leaves a gray rainy sky be-hind for darkness in the eight-mile tunnel. Twenty minutes later, the train breaks out of the hole in the mountain to clear sky and glistening snow. Trees heavy with snow. A bright blue and white world. Stop again to take off the electric engine and put back a waiting coal burner. (Until diesel replaced the smoky coal burners, electrical power was used to pull them through the long tunnel.)

Soon our five-hour ride ends as we slow to the Leavenworth depot. Then a short truck ride through Leavenworth up a dirt road, and we are back in the cozy house by the Icicle River, which Dorothy Bullitt had built for the family, for when school was out.

Mrs. MacDonald and her two boys, Robert and Kenneth, lived there and took care of the place. They also took care of the cows, the chickens, the vegetable garden, and a pig. The horses, in winter pasture, would return in the spring.

Mrs. MacDonald has the place warm now from the big stone fireplace; fragrance of chicken stew and apple sauce on the wood stove fills the air.

We kids sleep in the attic. Camp mattresses on army beds, under layers of gray wool blankets.

In the morning, the MacDonald boys are shoveling snow outside the doorway and clearing around the windows. It's been snowing a lot since Thanksgiving: snow fell last night; it's about five feet deep in the open. There's a steep trench now from floor level to the snow surface, so to get back into the house, we sit down and slide into the doorway.

"Hey Doug, let's go slide off the roof!" The two ten-year-olds go to the attic and get on a chair under one of the gabled windows. Snow on the roof is thick. It's slow to slide off the cedar shakes. Taking turns, each kid climbs out the window, the other gives a push, and down the roof, over the edge, and plop! Into the soft pile below.

Downhill skiing hasn't come to the West yet; it is only known in Europe. With a future to be of skiing, light snows, and metal roofs, roof sliding would soon pass into history.

Snowshoeing is what grownups do. Not for fun, but to get around, like for moving things or chopping a tree.

Midwinter around town is pretty quiet. Everyone appears

to be moving snow, shoveling roofs, and fixing plow blades. Children keep busy taking care of animals and bringing in wood and loads of sawdust, already stored from the mills near Peshastin to feed the simple burners at home. Without restaurants, social events are in churches and each other's homes; women make a lot of potlucks and everyone shares. Without much money to go around, neighbors trade services and food. Potlucks and sharing were, as they are today, a deeply imbedded part of Leavenworth culture.

Now that the Empire Builder is stopping again at Leavenworth, after forsaking us for so many years, each ride I take in the winter revives the memories connected with those familiar colors. The snow covering deep greens against a bright blue sky, the dark passage under the mountain, emerging into soft gray on the west, and then returning.

On looking back, through the eyes of a little girl on the train, it was an innocent time, one of simple delights to drop into the memory box.

Happiness then was made of snow, blue sky, family, and warm applesauce.

Thank you for sharing this trip with me. With Icicle Broadcasting Company, we wish all of you peace and harmony this Christmas midwinter season, in this most beautiful corner of the world.

It is obvious what a powerful memory and impact Leavenworth had on Harriet and how much she loved the Bullitt retreat on the shores of Icicle Creek.

Harriet's mother Dorothy Bullitt purchased approximately three hundred acres south of the city of Leavenworth out of a desire to find a retreat for herself and her three children after her husband, Harriet's father, died on April 10, 1932. In the book titled *Dorothy Simson Bullitt—An Uncommon Life*, author Delphine Haley writes,

> Dorothy managed to keep intact her own lifestyle and investments, while at the same time picking up more real estate at bargain prices. She began to look for a place to build a second home in a sunny, dry location near Seattle. She went about it in her special way using a mixture of method and intuition, studying maps, and taking time with people until she got what she wanted. In eastern Washington, she found the town of Leavenworth "one of the prettiest places I've ever seen, surrounded by the Cascade peaks and canyons carved by rushing rivers."

The following is again from Delphine Haley's book, and I think it is important to share this, as it illustrates the determination of Harriet's mother in finding exactly what she wanted in a family retreat. It is obvious that Harriet inherited the gift of determination from her mother, which served Harriet well to accomplish her work and dreams.

> Property regularly came up for auction as people either left or could not meet their obligations, and Dorothy watched for an attractive piece of land at an equally attractive low price. After renting a place in Leavenworth for a summer, she set her sights on an area south of town in a pine-sloped canyon cut by Icicle Creek. Over the next few years, she bought up acreage like pieces in a board game. She studied the ads for county sales. "I put as much land together as I could get and tried to make it into a package, but it didn't

matter because there was nobody else at the auction anyway."

The "little patch" eventually amounted to about three hundred acres, much of it bought for little more than a dollar an acre and obtained by varied and devious means.

She used similar tactics to secure the final acreage she wanted. After a long roadside "chat" with the reluctant owner, she suggested that if he didn't want cash, perhaps they could trade. "He looked past me and saw my car—a fancy little Ford convertible I had recently bought. So, I traded the car for the land and went home on the train."

⁂

Harriet shared that her mother developed Coppernotch in 1931 to 1932, right after my father died. Earlier, she would come over to Leavenworth with my father, taking horseback trips with Dude Brown. He was a well-known sheriff who owned and lived on the island. And he was also a wrangler. He took groups of people into the mountain backcountry and even on horseback trips to Stehekin. I think Mother wanted to have some ongoing contact and presence in the Icicle Creek area because it brought back memories of her husband, so she bought property here. Mother would go on the backpack trips, but Father often cut the trips short for a political meeting or had some other reason to get back to Seattle. Mother was never away as long as she wanted to be. She was frequently bored in Seattle, with my father always working on politics, but she knew he would be unhappy if he wasn't politically involved. She knew he would go off and do what he wanted, and he did. He was a political animal.

Nobody knows why the Coppernotch property and lodge was named Coppernotch. I asked Mother about the name, and she didn't know.

Maybe it was because of color of the hillside, or the copper pots all over the house, but we never knew the origin of the name.

My mother was born in Seattle. Her parents came out from the East. My grandfather was a lumberman from Michigan, and my grandmother was a music teacher. My grandfather came from a family of several boys. His father, my great-grandfather, logged with oxen. Grandfather told his boys to go west because they had logged most of the trees in the local area and because there was an unending supply of trees in the Northwest. He told one son to go to what is now Los Angeles and be ready to build houses and buildings. The other son, my grandfather, would go to the Northwest around Seattle, where he would cut trees, load them on a ship, and send the lumber to his brother to build Hollywood.

My grandparents and parents had a huge influence on me. My grandfather was an outdoorsman. He lost an arm when he was young to an infection from a sliver when cutting cord wood, and his arm had to be amputated. His mother had no mercy on him because of his handicap and expected him to behave like all the other boys and do all the same work. She knew he would have to face the world with this handicap as a working man. So he learned to cast a fly and play golf and shoot birds and sail a gaff rig yawl with top sails. Her father, with only one arm, was a lumberman running a sawmill, though he ended up supervising much of the time.

When he arrived in Seattle, he wanted a boat. He got his boat, and my mother spent a lot of time with her father sailing. Learning to swim, my mother was tied to the mast by a tether, and when it was time to swim, he put a life preserver on her and dropped her into the water and told her to swim. That had an big impact on her, because they both faced handicaps.

My mother had her own handicap—she was a woman. She was close to her father and enormously influenced by him. My siblings and I, as a result, were greatly influenced by our grandfather as well as our mother. My mother felt everything was available to her if she worked hard enough, and she taught us by example. The principal men in her life, her husband and grandfather, died in the same couple of years, and her mother died shortly after. She ended up inheriting an office building, the rather famous 1411 Fourth Avenue Building in downtown Seattle. It was initially built in 1928 for the Stimson Realty Company and in 1991 was listed on the National Register of Historic Places. My mother had never done anything but grow roses, go sailing, and enjoy the opera, and now she had this rather major business, and she was a woman. She couldn't even write a check or apply for a mortgage on this building, in the middle of the Depression. We children were very young at the time, so we grew up with nannies. Mother was a powerful, controlling person, but she adored us and wanted us to grow up right. We learned manners and personal care from our nanny. We learned how to carve out our future for ourselves by watching how our mother lived and worked and related to people. Mother was highly successful.

My paternal grandparents' house was near my mother's parents' home. I never knew my father's family. My father grew up in Louisville, Kentucky. He and my mother met at a wedding in Seattle. My mother's best friend married my father's brother, who lived in California, and he and my father came up for the wedding. My mother was the bride's maid of honor, and my father was his brother's best man, so they met in the wedding party. It was an instant love affair, and they were married about six weeks later. My mother was twenty-six years old, which in those days was almost over the hill for marriage. My father was about thirteen years older.

My father was a Southern Democrat in Louisville. In those days, the South was primarily Democratic. Democrats were the liberals, and he was into Louisville politics already; he was in some elected office. His older brother was a very conservative Republican who worked for President Taft. My father was glad to come to the Northwest.

Father took my mother back to Louisville when they were first married, but she couldn't stand it. His household was very religious. They pulled down the blinds on Sundays. They didn't allow any music; they had no dogs. It was shocking to us when she told us what that household was like. How could you live without a dog, and how could you pull the blinds down on Sunday? Didn't people go outside to play? Well, what did you do? Someone read the bible. So, Mother couldn't stand that very long, so she came back to Seattle. My father wanted to know if she was coming back to Louisville, and Mother said, "Never. If you love me, you will come to Seattle." So he did.

When he got to Seattle, he looked around and wondered where all the Democrats were. My father was an organizer. By trade, he was an attorney, but politics was in his blood. He discovered that Washington's state Legislature had only four Democrats, and the state Senate had none. He wondered what was wrong and knew something had to change, so he made it his career to organize the Democratic party before he died just a few years later. We grew up around the breakfast table talking politics.

He ran for office a couple of times, but as a vote-getter he was not very successful. As an organizer, though, he was successful, and he liked organizing. The Washington State Democratic Party today has its roots in what my father did back then. He got people together who could be leaders. Back in those days there were labor problems with the teamsters and the dock workers. He liked the working people. He made a lot of friendships by going down to the docks and talking with people who my mother considered rude and crude. Mother couldn't stand any of his friends.

My brother Stimson got involved with politics because of my father. Stimson loved to read, but he didn't like visiting with working people like my father did. My brother was an intellectual and a scholar, and he liked good company. He was very much hurt when my father died. They were close—or as close as you could be by age twelve. It was difficult to lose a father so young. I was seven. I was also affected by his death but didn't know it at the time. I felt so sorry for my mother who was now all alone.

I grew up in the Seattle Highlands, where our family was not popular socially. We were the only Democrats in the Highlands, a gated community. They were very proud of their golf course and their status, and we kind of dismissed all that. [For security reasons, the homes in the Highland did not have street addresses. Mail was simply addressed with the homeowner's name, The Highlands, Seattle, WA 98177. The Highlands had residents such as William Boeing, founder of The Boeing Company, the Nordstrom family, the Stimson families, and also Dorothy Bullitt, Harriet's mother.]

Originally there were fifty tracts of land in the Highlands. The Highlands sits 450 feet above the Puget Sound beaches, and we had to walk down the high bank to the west of the Highlands and across the railroad tracks to get to the beach. One of our earliest lessons was to stop, look, and listen before crossing the railroad tracks. I went to the beach with my sister and friends. We sometimes walked along the railroad tracks to Richmond Beach, and we were trusted to be careful. We would swim in Puget Sound. It was a rocky beach, but we didn't care. There were drift logs coming in all the time. We didn't mind the cold water. A lot of the summer was spent on the beach. The neighborhood was forested. We played outside all the time, and that delight is something I never lost.

Growing up in Seattle, we spent most of our time playing outdoors, climbing trees, and wishing there were a future for girl who climb trees. I only found out a few years ago there actually are opportunities for girls to climb trees and do research. We did a lot of swimming and sailing with friends. Everybody had sailboats or boats of some kind. There were no videos to watch or things to do in the house, and on a rainy day we would just wander around inside. We played outside all the time unless we were in school.

When we were at home as children, Mother wasn't like other mothers who taught their kids to make cookies and do domestic things. Sometimes I wanted to learn to cook. All I did was hang out in the kitchen and talk to our cook, but I wasn't really allowed to ask to help or learn. Mother thought that cooking and domestic things were unimportant, and that we should find something else to do. "You can always learn that later," Mother said. "After you get married you can learn all the domestic things."

Cooking was never big on my list of ambitions. As children, we had servants in the house, and our cook, as much as we loved her, didn't feel responsible for teaching us cooking techniques. I'd entertain myself sitting on the kitchen counter, sucking on an orange and stuffing a wad of bread with both butter and peanut butter into my mouth, watching her fry a fish or hamburger or boil some fresh peas (which I might have shelled). It didn't look complicated, but it was still mysterious. It was always good; we ate very well. We thought everybody did—except Armenian children. We were reminded every Sunday morning of how fortunate we were because elsewhere in the world children just like us were starving. Sometimes it was announced that we would not have Sunday morning waffles with maple syrup and melted butter because we were to consider the children who could not be so lucky (we wished we could provide waffles for those children but didn't know how).

My brother Stim and my sister Patsy were both older than me. I was closer to my sister growing up. They both ganged up on me when I was little, but they were always good friends to me. After my mother died, Patsy and I had a lot to do with the broadcasting company, so we saw each other often. We made decisions together. Since Stim was a lawyer we knew where to go to get legal advice.

My mother was the daughter of a logger, and she loved nature but thought it as a natural daily activity. She and my father spent time in Leavenworth and went on horseback trips, but in her day there was no such thing as environmental consciousness. Nature was the forest and

Puget Sound, and the outdoors was taken for granted, so saving the forest or Puget Sound was not an activity to become involved with. None of this was an issue in her day. My mother started the Bullitt Foundation, and it was modeled after what my grandmother started. My grandmother's causes were the orthopedic hospital, the arboretum, and the symphony. It was public health and the arts. Grandmother also supported the Cornish School. We kids could remember Miss Cornish—L.A.C. Cornish, a friend of Grandmother's. She helped Miss Cornish start the Cornish School. It was originally for drama, music, and dance.

Our garden and our grandparents' garden nearby yielded every vegetable and berry that thrived in the Seattle climate. There were three kinds of apple trees, three kinds of cherry trees, and the big golden plum, whose branches in late summer hung heavy with juicy rich fruits. Climbing that tree is a stellar memory today—biting into the taut skins swollen with sweet juice that ran down my chin. That's the way plums ought to be.

Mother's view for us was to "learn to cook later; not important. Whatever you do, do it well. If it's mud pies, make good ones." What was important to my mother was getting your education and speaking good English. Mother was involved with business, and she was very wrapped up in her work. She often talked about business and making decisions and how she worked with and dealt with men who dominated the business scene. She was on a couple of the boards for a bank and an insurance company, and she would talk about what it was like to be sitting in a room full of men and participating in decisions, and how you could get your thoughts and ideas across as a woman.

Mother was very soft-spoken, and she taught me to always look feminine but never send out sexual messages. Always go to the bathroom before a meeting, because as women we don't want to show weakness, and besides, you might miss something while in the bathroom. You should always do your homework to prepare for a meeting, and you always get to a meeting on time. Let men be late, because maybe they are out doing things with their children, like soccer. Women can never be late—men will think you are out shopping. The family lessons we had were about how to get along in society. The whole business in broadcasting was kind of imprinted on us. We weren't included in the business activities, but I couldn't miss the excitement involving the principles of doing something for the community and making money at the same time.

My mother was a major influence in my life, as were my children. Other people influential in my development include my fencing coach and later my flamingo dance instructor. Fencing was an important part of my life for ten years. It was significant for me because I got good at it. I was listed as one of the top ten competitors in the country—I came close going to the Olympics. Fencing is fighting. It is a killing game; it promotes aggression and requires thinking fast, and yet you don't hurt anybody. You can fight as hard as you like, but you still don't hurt anyone. It's all in good fun, but it is still serious. Growing up I was taught to hold back and not be aggressive. Fencing allowed me to learn how to be aggressive in a positive way, and also not to be hesitant for recognition of one's accomplishments.

Music was also part of my life growing up. The piano I have today is the same piano that was in our house where I was born and grew up, and I took piano lessons at a very young age. I practiced all my lessons and studies on that piano—it was a major piece in the living room in our house in the Highlands. (I lived in the Highlands until I went away to school and Mother sold the house.)

The piano was custom built for Fritz Kreisler, the famous musician, but he never used it and never even played it. Fritz Kreisler commissioned its construction—this was in New York. (Mother, as a young girl, lived in New York and studied music herself.) My mother was looking for a piano, and she wanted a good deal. She found this piano, custom-built and never picked up.

She learned that Fritz Kreisler had commissioned it himself from the

Mason & Hamlin Company. The German kaiser was in the middle of recruiting soldiers for the war—the First World War. Fritz Kreisler was German, and he had to go back to Germany to fight. He was already famous in the country, and the military made use of his extraordinary hearing. They sent him to the front lines and used his ability to locate enemy fire. (You can't imagine a more dangerous place to be or a situation that could more easily ruin his hearing.) He survived the war and came back to this country, but he never picked up the piano he commissioned.

Fritz Kreisler came back to this country after surviving the war and took up his musical career again. He had performances in Washington, DC, at a major concert hall, which was filled. At that time, the people in the East hated Germans because of the war. It was worse for the Germans in the East than in the West. When he went on the stage there were "boos" in the audience, and he didn't appear to notice at all. He picked up his violin and played through his whole concert, and when he finished the audience stood and roared in applause.

My mother got the piano because the factory sold it for a deal. It ended up in the living room at our home in the Highlands, and we lived with that instrument until we left home. Mother eventually gave it to me. The piano is now over a hundred years old. It's had some abuse over the years, and it's had some wear and tear, but it's traveled around to different places I've moved. We had it in the Sleeping Lady chapel for a while, and it was pushed back and forth. Most professional piano players don't want to play on this piano because it has a soft sound. They would rather play on the nine-foot Steinway. But I love the Fritz Kreisler piano because of its mellow tones. Fritz played the violin, and he probably didn't want his music to be overpowered by the piano. He didn't want to be upstaged by the piano. I wanted to restore the piano, and I put it in the hands of an expert restorer of pianos in Wenatchee, who restrung it. He also refinished the outside, so I now have a beautiful instrument in the living room of my new house, and I enjoy playing it.

I didn't do anything to emulate Grandmother, but music and art was part of my childhood. The outdoors we took for granted, enjoying the forest and the beach. My brother became interested in land acquisition through organizations like the Trust for Public Lands, and Stim changed the purpose of the Bullitt Foundation, which was initially oriented as a service organization in Seattle. My mother was not what you would call an environmentalist, although she thought it was terrible when she became aware of the destruction that was happening. But she wasn't part of any advocacy organization, though my brother was. It was Stimson who reoriented the Bullitt Foundation as an environmental advocacy foundation. He got the foundation to make the first acquisition of wilderness land. They spent lot of money buying land, and the foundation's resources got pretty thin. So the foundation morphed into environmental action. When I came back to Seattle in 1963, I gave the foundation more of a push. Whatever participation I had with meetings, I leaned more toward saving wildlands and forests, and my sister went along with it. She grew up in the same way, in the woods and beaches, and she thought that was all important. But my brother had the lead, and my mother went along with his emphasis. My mother was old-fashioned; she thought women should be secretaries. Mother was not a feminist at all. She hired men who were qualified. She didn't try to give opportunities to women. My brother discovered Jean Enersen for KING Radio and gave her a good job. Jean developed into an award-winning KING TV reporter.

Stim hired women because he believed in that principle, and he looked for qualified women. Our mother didn't, but she expected her daughters to do anything they wanted to do. She encouraged us, but she knew it was hard because of her personal experience. She had to carve her place in society. She felt all the discriminations. She felt all the men she worked with in her life were demeaning her, and they were. But she found a way of getting respect. She found she was smarter than most of the men, but she was clever enough not to show it. She made sure she wouldn't upstage any of them. She taught us that, when we were meeting with men, we should never be seductive and never try to upstage them. Before going into a meeting, you should determine your desired outcome and then make sure that it occurs. There are always techniques to reach your outcome. Always let the men *have* the ideas, but make sure the ideas are yours. Mother would always wear a ruffle around her neck so she looked like a woman. She was disgusted by women who dressed like men. Mother had a very boring wardrobe, low key clothing but nice jewelry. She was always very feminine. She could have been hit on by all the guys. She was a sexy lady, but she downplayed it. She imposed her dress standards on her daughters. She told us not to smoke—not because of a health concern, but rather that it did not look good for women to smoke. Smoking was not ladylike. Mother said, "If you want to smoke, smoke at home—here is a cigarette." We all tried it but didn't like it, and I never smoked.

When we were growing up, we were taught modesty and not to show off. My grandparents were the type who would not promote anyone getting on stage and showing off. They would gladly entertain people who were on stage, but you don't do that yourself. You don't show your body, you don't show your emotions; you control your emotions. That was our household. You didn't show grief or show elation. Perhaps this was a British influence. It took a sport like fencing for me to get out and discover I could be really conspicuous. I could have a lot of fun, and people could watch me. That was particularly useful to me in later life. I learned to be a showoff.

We considered the people in the Highlands conservative Neanderthals from big corporations. They all had lots of money. They all belonged to the golf club. I guess they were spin-offs of my grandparents' friends. We were the children of a Democratic organizer and sometimes felt on the outs. It was obvious to us we were members of the wrong political party. My father died when we were very young. We just had the stamp of being Democrats. It wasn't any handicap; we weren't outcasts. We just really didn't like the company we were in. The community didn't accept anyone that wasn't like them. No Black persons or Jewish persons could ever buy property in the Highlands at that time.

We grew up talking around the breakfast table about civil rights, equality for all, equal labor practices, more pay for women, keeping children out of the mines, and all those things that my father was connected with, and we thought the whole neighborhood was pretty backward. The community thought we were a bunch of radical rabble-rousers. We didn't care. Actually, we were all friends. We went to the same church—a very traditional Episcopalian church. It was a gift from Horace Henry and dedicated as a memorial to his daughter Florence Henry, and it was located right in the Highlands. C.D. Stimson donated the Kimbell pipe organ to the church. It was a beautiful little stone chapel. I was married in that chapel. Everybody went to church, and everybody knew each other. We were very much socially a part of the community, but we were kind of disgusted with their attitudes. The Depression was rampant at that time, and all the work projects like the Civilian Conservation Corp (CCC), the Tennessee Valley Authority, and the Works Progress Administration put people to work and helped a lot with the Depression. All the people in this neighborhood hated all these programs because they cost money, but they did help put people to work. The government should have a CCC program now, in this time. It worked back then. The Coulee Dam project came along, and that put young men to work. (Young women didn't work. Most young women didn't even go to college.)

My father was appointed by the Governor of Washington State to serve on a committee dealing with labor problems. He died of cancer on April 10, 1932 at the age of fifty-five, and the governor appointed my mother to take his place on the committee. There was a group in the state that wanted the commission dissolved, so they pinpointed my mother as the easiest one to get rid of, since she was a woman. But they didn't know my mother. They threatened to kidnap us children. Those opposing the work of this committee thought Mother would be an easy one to pick off; even Mother thought that. Mother was the only one who was threatened. I don't think the men on the committee were.

Because of the threats against Mother, there were bars on our house windows, and a watchman came every night. He was so tall he had to duck going through the door, and he wore a gun. He walked around the house all night, I guess, and then he checked out in the morning. That was when we were driven everywhere, and we kids thought it was so exciting that we could fool the kidnappers. We were told not to talk with any strange men, but we weren't grounded to the house. We were just told to be careful, so it turned into a game for us. My friend and I would run around the woods and fantasize what kidnappers looked like. We thought the kidnappers must be boogiemen carrying burlap bags around with chloroform rags, looking for little children. We would climb the tallest trees and spend our playtime watching for kidnappers.

This was long before KING Broadcasting was started. There had been some major kidnappings at the time, such as the Lindberg baby, who was killed. The heir to the Matson Shipping Line, a baby, was also kidnapped and brutally killed, and then George Weyerhaeuser, when he was a child, was kidnapped but returned safely. He was out on the back porch of their Tacoma home and was snatched right off the porch. His life was threatened, but they found him and got him back. He grew up to run the Weyerhaeuser Corporation.

Mother, of course, was alarmed by the kidnapping threat involving us, so that's why we had bars on the windows and the night watchman. During the time we were under threat of kidnapping, we had to be driven to school. Even though the Cornish School, where we took music lessons, was only a short distance from our regular school, the driver was required to pick us up and drive us to the lessons. We were never allowed to be on the street by ourselves. We thought that this was so exciting.

I was seven when my father died, so I must have been eight or nine during the kidnapping scare. Father never lived to see Franklin D. Roosevelt elected president. Father ran Roosevelt's Washington State campaign but never lived to see the election. He had been Roosevelt's friend and worked for him in various ways in the earlier days, and he worked for all the campaign platforms relating to his public works projects, along with major efforts repealing prohibition. Father was a Southern Democrat from Kentucky and thought prohibition was ridiculous.

He also fought to eliminate child labor. Children were being sent into the coal mines. Women were being paid next to nothing. And so Roosevelt had platforms to reform all these things and get labor unions more money. Father was friendly with the guys on the docks and the people who worked on the ferry boats and ships that came into the harbor. Mother thought they were all pretty crude and rough. She also didn't understand how Father could stand the abuse he was getting from the Republicans.

Father ran for congress and governor and was defeated for both positions. His success was in organizing, not getting votes. There were basically no Democrats in the state before Father arrived. My grandparents were Republicans. They weren't politically active, but they were conservative people from the logging business, one of the richest families in the area. Mother was from a conservative and religious Protestant family. Then my father came on the scene to be with my mother, and my grandparents liked him. They didn't agree with him, but he was a charmer. He was nice to everyone. In those days conservative Republicans weren't like they are today. They were generally financially responsible people, and they didn't want things to change too fast.

I think of my father's situation often these days. Mother would go to all my father's speeches, and then people would bombard him with horrible criticism. People hated him, but many more people loved him. When Father got this horrible criticism, Mother would say, "How do you stand those people? They say such bad things about you. How can you stand it, it must hurt you?"

We went to school in the Highlands from kindergarten to the fifth grade. It was a little schoolhouse with a swimming pool, and they always held Christmas parties. The schoolhouse was one big room that could be divided by an accordion wall. We had two teachers, one full-time and one part-time art teacher. The main teacher taught the traditional subjects and put together Christmas plays, but didn't do anything special in terms of nature. Nature was just the way we lived. Trees to climb. No video games or computers. Nothing to do inside except practice the piano. We got home from school, put on old clothes, and went outside to play. We played outdoors all the time. Playing outdoors was what kids did.

There was a grocery store on 145th Street. We would walk out of the Highlands past the golf course and go to the store where we could buy bubble gum and ice cream bars for a nickel.

After the fifth grade we went to St. Nicholas School close to downtown Seattle, attending grade six through grade ten. St. Nicholas School was a private nonsectarian girls' school founded in 1910 and located in Seattle's Capitol Hill neighborhood. The school was named to honor St. Nicholas, the patron saint of children, but had no religious affiliation. Attended by the children of many of Seattle's leading families, St. Nicholas School strove to provide its students with an education that would both prepare them to pursue higher education and equip them to proceed comfortably into Seattle's upper-class society. In 1917, the school was sold to a group of parents—members of Seattle's leading families, including the Stimson family. At St. Nicholas School you could go to the office and buy a big Hersey bar for a nickel.

From St. Nicholas School we would walk to Cornish School. Then we were picked up, and it was a half hour drive home to the Highlands. (The Cornish School was started by Nellie Cornish and was initially located in the Booth Building at Broadway and Pine on Capitol Hill.) Nellie Cornish had a motherly manner, warmth and generosity, a sparkling eye, a quick wit, and enormous energy. Cornish was recognized as having special talent for teaching music to youngsters, and many Seattle families put their children under her tutelage for an arts education beyond what the public schools could offer.

A Japanese driver worked for our parents. In those days there were no service stations, so if you had a car you had to service it yourself. Our family had a garage with a pit in the floor to work underneath the vehicle, and we also had a shop full of tools. The car was kept in good operating condition. Our mechanic was also an expert driver and drove us everywhere, especially when Mother received those threats about kidnapping. The Japanese employee was our mechanic until the Japanese people in the Northwest were interned at the beginning of World War II. Our employee and his entire family were picked up in the middle of the night. Mother went ballistic when she heard they'd been picked up, and she found out where they were sent. She immediately went to Idaho to the internment camp and got the entire family out. She sent them back East to stay with the family of Dr. Harold Amos.

Mother had met the Amos family because Harold, their son, was a classmate of my brother Stimson. The Amos family home was in Connecticut. Mother thought our employee and family would be safe in Connecticut, because on the East Coast they hated the Germans, but they weren't fearful of the Japanese. Our employee and his family eventually came back to Seattle, and Mother got one of them a job at the children's hospital. By the time they returned to Seattle, people didn't need mechanics anymore, since there were gas stations on every corner.

CHAPTER 2
Leaving Home—Struggling with Education

———∞∞———

AFTER ATTENDING ST. NICHOLAS SCHOOL through grade ten, Mother arranged for me to go back East to a boarding school. There were no questions, no options. That is where I would go. She sent all three of us children to boarding school. I think she was tired of dealing with teenage problems. She was trying to get into a profession herself. Life was pretty hard for her in a man's world, trying to run a business and having three teenagers in the house. She was first involved with the real estate business with the 1411 Fourth Avenue Building. Later she started a radio station, a television station, and the new KING FM classical music station. We were gone by then.

The boarding school was named Chatham Hall, an all-girls college preparatory boarding school located in Chatham, Virginia. It was a religious school, but it wasn't strict. We went to church a lot. Vesper services were held every evening, and they had Sunday church services. The mission of Chatham Hall was to prepare girls for college and for productive lives. Its rigorous educational program encouraged intellectual growth, creativity, and personal responsibility. The school is grounded in its episcopal heritage. The rector was the principal of the school, and he had been a school friend of my father. My mother found out who he was and prevailed on him to take me into the school. I was a really bad student.

I ended up at the bottom of the class, but I graduated anyway. Mother never came to my graduation, which was disappointing to me, but she was really busy.

I was living in a dream world, and I recall I didn't care. Chatham Hall really didn't have subjects that were of interest to me. They didn't provide physics or math or astrophysics. They only had one year of math and one year of chemistry, and those were the things I liked. They had a lot of history, and English and Latin and other languages. My French teacher didn't like me. She only liked the girls who were serious about learning French, and I wasn't. I didn't like history and hated Latin. They had a required an athletic program. Everyone had to play field hockey, and I resisted because we had to wear awful uniforms. I said, "I'm not going to do that." I was kind of rebellious. I didn't see why I should run all the way to the end of the field and then run back, so I said, "I'm not going to do that," and they didn't know what to do. A couple of other girls followed suit. The other girls said that they didn't want to do that either, so there was a little cluster of us that didn't want to play field hockey. They said, "Well you have to do something. So, what can you do? You can hike on Saturdays all day." We hiked about five miles, rain or shine. I had a raincoat, and it didn't bother me to hike in the rain, since I came from Seattle. We went out and we hiked really fast and we had a picnic; we had a good time. The Virginia countryside is beautiful with all the red pines, and it was good exercise. I think they felt it should be punishment and that we shouldn't like it, but we enjoyed it and continued to hike for our athletic program. I didn't want to be at Chatham Hall. I wanted to be home and go to school where I had friends.

The school also had horses, and you could take training with horses. I had ridden horses in Seattle, but it was English riding at Chatham Hall. We took beautiful rides: moonlight rides and breakfast rides with a picnic breakfast that somebody made. We had chases and hunts, not with animals but with someone riding ahead, and I learned jumping. There horses were well trained, and that was a fun time, riding and learning more about riding. I also had riding lessons growing up at home in Seattle, so it was a familiar thing to do.

But at Chatham, I was living in a dream world, being a mediocre student. I didn't end up well. I didn't make an impression on any colleges that Mother wanted me to consider, to her consternation. She hoped I would go to Vassar. Mother even took me to Vassar for an interview, and I said, "No, thank you." I looked like an idiot, and they looked at my record and said no.

I decided to go back to the University of Washington. At that time anybody could go to the university if they were residents of the state, and it was very low cost. I was interested in engineering. I took math and physics. I thought I wanted to be a chemical engineer, so I took all the chemistry and math in the first years and was admitted to the engineering college. I wasn't a terrific student, but I liked it.

They banished me from using the library, which was a very hurtful experience. I worked hard to get into the engineering school. I had to qualify with a certain level of math. It took me a year taking chemistry, and I worked hard to meet those requirements. In the first year of the engineering curriculum I had to take drafting and drawing and learn to letter, and I did all that, but it was hard. They required us to draw certain things, and I didn't even know what they were. I didn't have a father to tinker with me like the boys did. I used the library a lot because I could learn details of what we were drawing. One assignment was to draw the moving parts inside a drill press. Everyone else in the class were boys, and they didn't have any problem with that. I didn't know what a drill press was or what it looked like, let alone what the inside looked like, so I needed the library. I wasn't doing well, and the professor didn't like me being the only girl in the class. I did my best, but it was hard for me. It was all unfamiliar territory.

But on one occasion, I was in the library, and the head of the physics department came in and took me into his office and sat me down. He made it clear I was not to use the library in the future. I asked why not, and he said these boys were all serious students and registered in ROTC, a military program in the college. He emphasized that when these boys got their degree, they would be in the military service. He said that the boys really had to succeed, and that they were serious, and that having a girl in the class was distracting, so he asked me never to come back to the library. There was no affirmative action program at that time. If it would have been like it is now, I would have raised holy hell, but on that day all I could do was go down the hall in tears and tell my mother that I couldn't use the library. I didn't know who to complain to. There was no possibility of putting in a complaint about the way I was treated. (Some years later my mother was on the Board of Regents at the University of Washington, but at this time she had no influence or power.)

I had no options, so after they made it so uncomfortable for me in the engineering classes, and since I wasn't doing sufficiently well in the class to oppose them, I withdrew and decided I'd go to the upper campus and do "what girls do." I'm going to forget this life that boys have access to, and I'm never going back. I'm going to do what girls do, so maybe I can succeed at something. I went and changed my whole curriculum and signed up for home economics. That's what girls do. I'd take home economics and stenography, and I'd learn to work in an office and cook because that is what girls do. "I'll really stick it to them," I thought, but I stuck it to myself, giving up what I really wanted to do.

I'd join a sorority, which I was against in principle, but I did decide to join anyway. I signed up for rushing at the Kappa Kappa Gamma house, because that is where all my friends were. I didn't take part in any of the activities. They had expectations—pledges had to maintain a certain level of scholarship, and I never became a member because my scholarship wasn't good enough.

I found a friend that also wanted to take home economics, and she also had to take a gym class, which was another requirement for us. I couldn't take swimming because I had previously taken all levels of swimming classes. My friend and I choose the thing we least wanted to do, which was golf. We ended up taking home economics and golf, and we were total disasters at both. But we had fun giggling.

Golf wasn't bad. The golf pro liked us. We took a couple of lessons learning to hit the ball and how to swing the club, and then the golf pro turned us loose on the course. The course was where the university medical school is now. It's now completely covered with the medical buildings. The golf course was all green, and we thought we could take an hour and walk around the course without doing anything, since they weren't watching us. We giggled and told jokes as we walked the course. We got graded on what the pro taught us in the first lessons on hitting the ball.

The home economics class was in a huge laboratory. Everybody had a place at the counter, and the instructor gave us the first edition of *The Joy of Cooking*, our textbook. The title of the class was "Feeding the Family in Wartime." It was wartime, and this book was all about recipes with low sugar and low fat, because you couldn't get sugar and fat, as it was rationed. It was all on feeding your family nourishing food that didn't cost very much money and provided healthful dining. This was in the early 1940s. Today they are back to the same thing in new cookbooks, plus what you can grow in your own garden. They are again encouraging low sugar diets and meals that won't make you fat. But at that time, cooking involved leaving out the things that were rationed because you couldn't buy them. Oatmeal and stewed prunes—that was no problem for me because that's what we had all along at home. It was easy, and we bluffed our way through.

There were no surprises until we had to make French toast. I loved French toast. It was a big treat at home. We had it on Sunday mornings, with lots of butter and maple syrup, and I thought, "This is going to be fun." I got my bread from the egg mixture in the frying pan and started cooking, and immediately the professor came along and whipped the skillet out of my hand and took it up to the front of the room. She stopped the whole class and said, "Class, I want you to see what you should never do. This is the worst mistake you can possibly make." I began to shrink smaller and smaller, and my friend was chuckling. I had allowed my bread to soak too long: a huge catastrophe, because I had made soggy French toast, and it all fell apart in the pan. The professor said, "I want to show you what you can do when you let the bread soak too long in the eggs—never do this." She made it sound as if it was a horrible thing.

She said, "Now, I'm going to show you, if this should ever happen, what you can do so as not to waste it, because we never waste anything. The solution to this experience is you muddle it up in the pan—it's already soggy anyway. You just stir it around," and then she took out a jar of marmalade, "and you cover the mixture with marmalade." And then she took a muffin tin and she put a little bit of the butter in the tin and then spooned the soggy mixture into the muffin tin and heated it and said, "Then you put it in the oven, and you roast it for a while, and now you have a beautiful bread pudding. This is what you do if you have an accident with French toast, and you can save everything and throw nothing away." So that was the lesson how to make bread pudding, which I have never made and never will. But I've made successful French toast ever since because I never leave it too long in the egg mixture. I ended up with an incomplete in that class because I never took the written exam.

The fact that my mother was well known in the business community didn't have any impact on the way I was treated. I was just a girl along with the other girls. My mother had her own feud with the university but for different reasons. At the time I attended, there was no family familiarity. I didn't graduate from the University of Washington at that time, since I had done so poorly. I got incomplete in the home economics course. I had dropped out of the engineering school. I only lasted two days in the stenography class, because we had to learn how to make these little signs on paper. These were certain symbols, and when I looked at the symbols, they didn't look any different from handwriting, so what's the difference? So I left the stenography class.

Then along came Leslie Denmon, my best friend, who I grew up with. She was attending Bennington College, in Bennington, Vermont, and she was having a wonderful experience. She said, "Harriet, you're not doing so well at the university, so why don't you apply at Bennington? You would really like it here. It is a smaller rural college, and there are all kind of things. You can work on the farm, and you can take any classes you want." I replied that they will never take me because my grades are so bad, but she said they don't rely much on grades. "Why don't you just apply?" So I did apply, and they took me. I was surprised because other colleges didn't want me. I went to Bennington, and that was probably my best experience. I got into premed. Engineering was in the past. I would rather take something that had to do with life forms. For the premed curriculum, I took biology, embryology, and bacteriology. Bennington didn't give grades, just comments, and it was nice to have no grades. Bennington College was founded in 1932 as a women's college and later became coeducational. But I learned afterward that, without grades, it was difficult to transfer into another school.

Chapter 3
Moving Forward in Life

───── ∞ ─────

I met Bill Brewster, a Dartmouth Boy, on a double date with my friend. We fell in love and were married. While Bill and I were living in New York, we decided to get our pilot's licenses, as we felt claustrophobic. We were both from county backgrounds, and living in New York was sort of mentally crushing. It was a six-hour drive to Jones Beach, and to go to New England and get to any ski places we had to drive four hours. You don't take many trips under those circumstances. Bill was interning and then taking a residency to finish his medical training, and I was working in a laboratory for two women researchers, working on chronic kidney disease. This work was with rats, so I took care of a lot of rats. I really enjoyed the babies. Rats can get accustomed to being handled by people.

We began to think creatively as to what we could do to get out of the city, and we concluded we would learn to fly. We could cross over the bridge over the Hudson River into New Jersey. In Hackensack there was a base where we could learn to fly seaplanes, so both of us took lessons. The lessons themselves were fun. We got through the first phase, where we both flew solo and then took cross-country trips working toward the private license. The instructor establishes a route for you to learn navigation and designated how many miles you would fly. We took separate airplanes, and we flew all over the place, up the Hudson River and to Connecticut, using navigation maps they supplied. However, we didn't finish the requirements for our private licenses. Years later, when I moved back to Seattle, I completed my private license on Lake Union with Kenmore Air. I didn't have a whole lot more time, but I was determined to at least get my private license.

Because Bill was in the military, we ended up in Frankfurt, Germany. I decided to attend Heidelberg University. It provided something to do as an alternative to staying around the military compound, where officers' wives were just sitting around. I had two little babies, but it was easy to get nursemaid help and be away for the day. The American Forces had the use of the train going from Frankfurt to Heidelberg, so I decided I would go to the university and learn German. In Frankfurt I really didn't need German, because we lived in the military compound, surrounded by Americans.

The Germans were not only defeated, they were crushed. The buildings in Frankfurt were half destroyed from bombs, and there was a huge financial depression in the country. They were defeated and they didn't seem to understand why. They had put their faith in a leader, and they felt betrayed. Here they were living in rubble, and they couldn't get food. A lot of men had died, and the families were struggling with little or no help.

Getting to Heidelberg on the commuter train wasn't a problem. I just followed what I was told to get accepted into the university. I went to an advisor, whom I later learned knew and understood English, but he wasn't talking to me in English; he spoke to me very quietly and politely in German. He told me I shouldn't start by taking just one course and a couple of German classes but that I should go into the whole medical curriculum, whether I understood it or not. I really didn't know what he was saying, because I didn't know German. He took me down to registration to get me admitted. The tuition they wanted was four cartons of cigarettes and a couple of pounds of coffee. It was a total black market economy. Cigarettes were the cash. Money was no good—you could just throw that away. I went back to Frankfurt to the military post exchange and purchased a collection of cigarettes and coffee, and I took it back to the registrar at Heidelberg. They were happy to get it and registered me for all the classes. I had a crash course in German from the students and they signed me up for the non-German speakers. There were classes in beginner, intermediate, and advanced German, and they signed me up to take all of them. Some days I had a class in all three levels, and it was the best language course that I have ever seen, because it was all in German.

The other students in the classes were mostly men. The people who wanted to learn German in the university were not native Germans. They were all from the Eastern countries—Czechoslovakia, Hungary, and Romania; all the countries that were also defeated. They could all speak enough German to communicate with each other, so German was a common language. There were Estonians, Latvians, and Lithuanians. Everybody could speak a little bit of Russian, too, enough to connect with each other, but they all spoke bad German. But I could speak no German, and we were all in the same class.

The class was all storytelling. The professor got up in front of the class to tell very simple stories, and then we were to write down what we remembered from the stories. That was a huge challenge, but it was such a good way of teaching. We weren't translating everything into English. No one in the room could speak any English. They were all speaking a little bit of German. I learned to understand through these stories.

I learned German from other students too because they would ask me a lot of questions. They didn't know any English. They wanted to know things from me that I wasn't used to talking about. Somebody would ask something like, "In America, when you are in church, what is the preacher allowed to say?" And I said, "Well, anything." They didn't believe me. They said that can't be. They could not believe that there weren't some terrible rules about what you could say in church. These countries were all autocracies, and they had to be careful about what they said. I would try and convince them, but then I didn't know sufficient German to do so.

They would ask questions like, "Why are you Americans so bad to your Negros?" and I would say, "That's a good question," and then counter with, "Why are you so prejudiced against Polish people?" because they hated the Poles. They would say, "You don't understand; it is a completely different situation. Poles are very bad people." And they would say the same thing about the French, the French are really bad people, but they didn't see anything bad about Negros, so why were we so hard on them?

These conversations made me go back to my dictionary, and I would study on the train, phrases and words, but I didn't study the grammar, because I didn't think the grammar mattered. I didn't care about the gender and the verb forms. I just wanted to be able to talk. I didn't care if the grammar was bad. I could learn that later.

I noticed some people at the base in Frankfurt had learned German in college. Some people even had degrees in German language, but they never talked to anybody in German. They would find people who could speak English, like the servants or the people taking care of the Americans. They spoke English, and they expected English to be spoken to them.

The Germans always wanted to try out their English. I wanted to keep talking to people in German, and it was really hard, but it was the best way to learn. Just forget about the grammar and just talk, and after while the rhythm of the language and certain combinations of words set in, and you just absorbed it. It wasn't from studying it but from hearing the same combinations again and again, so I finally learned to speak it. I got pretty good after a while. I could talk to anyone about anything. I never got the genders right, but I don't think it mattered.

Some of the students were from Eastern Europe and had skills, not necessarily skills they could use in their own country but skills they could sell when they escaped into Germany. One couple I met left Hungary. The husband had been in the Hungarian Army. I think he said he was a colonel and also a polo player in the Olympics. He was good at fencing. I don't know if he ever taught fencing, but it was something people learned in these countries. I guess he had learned and competed, so he had the skill. He also trained horses. When the Russians approached on one side of Hungary and the Germans approached on the other, his military duty had been to protect the industrial fabric of machinery from being dismantled. I guess the Germans tried to dismantle all the equipment, and he was trying to keep it together for Hungry. His job ended at the end of the war. General Patton was coming in from the German side, and Patton was told to stop before entering Hungary. I think Eisenhower was behind the decision that American Forces were not to go all the way into Hungary; the people who lived there hated the Germans, of course. The Germans had occupied Hungary. All those countries hated the Germans.

But they were terrified of the Russians. So when they saw the Russians coming at them from the East, they, like so many others, had to make a decision, and decided to go with the Germans into Austria. I guess they got into a displaced persons camp. They got over the border in the dark of night on Christmas Eve, and they ended up in Heidelberg. He got a job with US Special Services and handled all the entertainment and athletic opportunities for service men. He also taught fencing, so that's what he was doing at the University of Heidelberg. He would give a lesson to anyone who would pay $5.

I didn't have any particular interest in fencing, but I had a friend who did. She was the daughter of an American colonel in Frankfurt, and I got to know her. I think she was from Florida. She was about my age, and she didn't have anything to do either. I was at the university all day, and the commuter train came in the morning and went back at night, so I spent all day there and had some classes with time in between. My friend was also taking the same classes. I don't think she could speak German either. She suggested we take fencing. It was something new to learn, so we went together and signed up for lessons. We both took lessons at the same place and time, and it was fun. At first it was just exercise, but fencing eventually became a big part of my life.

———— ∞∞ ————

When it was time to go back to the United States, we went to Boston. Bill had a job at Massachusetts General as an anesthesiologist. I continued fencing in America. There was a big fencing club in Boston, and they held competitions. New York was the central place where they had strong fencing groups and competitions on a national level.

After a year or two I started to go to New York for lessons, because I was improving. A guest from Yugoslavia came along. He was a friend of the fencing master at MIT, whom I'd gotten to know. His MIT group and the one I belonged to went back and forth and did some competing. There were mostly men and only one woman. Later, I joined the MIT group.

The fencing master at MIT was also Yugoslavian, and he came to me one day and said he had a companion back in Yugoslavia who had a scientific theory. He speaks only German; no English. He had worked in General Tito's army in radio communications and was one of Tito's activists. He had this theory of the universe, how planets and other bodies revolve around each other due to electromagnetism and gravity, and his wonderful theory explained how the bodies remain in orbit. He told me this man was a very nice guy, and he was also a very good fencer. He was looking for a place where this guy could live, since he didn't have room in his apartment. He wanted his friend to live with us.

Bill was busy working all day, and we had a house with a guest room, and I said he could live with us. The fencing master said, "Perhaps you could translate his theory because you know some German. He will tell you what his theory is all about, and you will translate it into English."

Stupid me. What we got was a hornet's nest.

He was this very studious-looking man, and he brought his fencing equipment and his theory in this big satchel. He would be pleased to give me fencing lessons. We had some space in the house, and we could go out into the driveway to practice every day.

He built me a fencing model on the back of a door. The model was something like an arm with a hand that held a foil, and it would spring back and forth so I could practice. It had a target that was the same distance of a person's target zone, so it was marvelous for me to practice with. It was a cleverly crafted thing, and I used it all the time. I could practice all my motions, and every day I worked at it, adjusting my distance. It wasn't like sparring a real person, but it was a drill, and I could work on this drill by myself.

This fellow experienced a deep depression. We wanted to help him and, we did get him to the hospital and offered an extended stay, since he wanted to come back to us. The doctors told us he was schizophrenic and seriously paranoid. While on medication he was very calm and apologetic about the problems he had caused us.

After several weeks he became depressed and paranoid again, and the doctors urged him to return to Yugoslavia. He agreed to leave and got passage on a flight. His companions didn't want anything to do with him. We got him on the airplane and never heard from him again. I often wondered what happened to him. I continued using the fencing practice device he made.

I was still taking lessons and going to New York to work with a fine trainer nearly every week. I had the time, and I joined the club in New York and had an opportunity to play with some of the top people in the country. New York and LA were where the best fencing clubs in the

United States were located.

I began working up in the competition. I won the New England sectional championship and then got into the all-Eastern championship and placed. Then I went into the New York City Metropolitan championship which was the most difficult. You need to be excellent just to get through the preliminaries. I ended up as a ranking winner in the top ten because I placed in the national championship. I never won first, but I got into the finals and placed in the first six. Because of that record, I was asked to join the Olympic squad to compete. They would take two competitors and a runner up. I was the fourth.

It was a good experience. It taught me to be assertive. The people who won were really smart and could watch me and figure out my game. They knew how to win, but I had a couple of things I did well.

———— ⚬≫≪⚬ ————

Bill and I eventually moved to Florida. Bill had a tough time with alcohol. He had a medical friend in Florida who helped him get a job. I also wanted to work so I had something to do beyond family activities.

One of my jobs was working in a laboratory in Florida where we milked rattle snakes for their venom. It was also my job to feed the snakes live mice. The lab was studying the effects of venom on blood cells. The lab had government funding, and they wanted to know the component of the venom that caused massive hemorrhaging. They wanted to know what breaks down and bursts open the red blood cells. That was my job.

There are a lot of snakes in Florida. The ones we primarily worked with were the eastern diamondback rattlesnakes, which are big. In the wild they can be rather aggressive, but in captivity they tend to be more lethargic, and I could handle them. The water moccasins were so big and strong; I let one of the men handle them.

While we were in Florida, we attended an Episcopal church to be involved in the community and meet more people. This turned out to be one of my more disappointing experiences. I discovered that this particular congregation refused to allow a Black family to attend. A group of us in the congregation decided to leave and start another group associated with the Episcopal church. We got permission to meet in another Protestant church nearby, but it turned out that that church again refused to allow Blacks to attend. That was the end of my association with any organized church organizations. It didn't make sense to me for any church to segregate their membership. This didn't meet any of my understanding of the Bible and the message Jesus shared.

Because Bill could not deal with his alcohol problem, I made the decision to leave the marriage and to move back to Seattle with my children, where I had family and friends. My son Scott was born in Boston, and my daughter Wenda was born in Frankfurt, Germany. When we came back from Germany, the children were two and three years old, and initially there were some happy times in my first marriage with their father. The marriage had a happy beginning, but eighteen years later it ended in divorce. The children finished their education in Seattle.

CHAPTER 4
Returning to Seattle

⎯⎯⎯ ⚭ ⎯⎯⎯

I RETURNED TO SEATTLE AFTER the divorce and decided to again register at the University of Washington. I had never finished my college education. It took me a long time to scrape together enough courses to have a transcript, so at the age of forty, after a long life of motherhood, working, and living a very different life, I came back to Seattle as a single mom.

I got a degree in zoology, which I thought for me would be the easiest. Zoology wasn't hard, and it was a joy to take the classes with a lot of field work on the beaches, in the forests, and in the river valleys. It was interesting stuff, and I loved it. It was probably the foundation for the resources I had for starting the *Pacific Search* magazine, with all the zoology contacts I'd made and the nature study involving snakes and frogs and all the invertebrates on the beach.

It bothered me that there was a lot of destruction during field trips, because there was no education in conservation ethics. Students were being turned loose with their buckets on the pristine rocky beaches, turning over rocks and bringing all kinds of invertebrates home, where they would die. With such a large number of students, there was destruction on the beaches.

Through uncontrolled logging, forests were being taken down without much common sense. Since there were so many resources, the general public thought they weren't being destroyed, but they were. That was the incentive to start a magazine to talk about these things. There was a chance that publishing would become my next career.

I ended up without much faith or respect for the education system in the United States. I thought of continuing on for a PhD in zoology or biochemistry, but it was difficult, and I didn't think I was capable or smart enough or actually had the commitment to follow through; I probably wouldn't stick to it. I wanted to get busy doing something, but I would have liked to go on for an advanced degree.

Since I was interested in a number of things such as zoology and nature, I decided I would go out and find other people who could contribute to a nature journal about zoology. I knew good people who were interested in this, so I decided to start the zoology and nature journal. It became a magazine that featured the nature and natural history of the Pacific Northwest. No one else was doing this.

I started *Pacific Search* from scratch. It began as a volunteer production for the Seattle Science Center. I needed to associate it with an institution of some kind to give it some credibility. I tried to get it based at the Burk Museum, but they weren't interested. So I went to the Science Center, and the director, Dixie Lee Ray, thought it was a great idea. I wanted it sent out to different environmental groups, since this magazine was to be a cross-connect between different environmental groups. They had their own newsletters, but my theory was that they would like to be connected with other groups. This could be a collaboration of all the groups, with the theory that people who like birds would also like wild flowers, and those same people would be interested in rocks and mountains and vertebrates on the beach and the lizards in eastern Washington and would like to read about all those things. That's what this journal was to be about.

The groups would subscribe to the magazine and agree to take a certain number of copies. That was our first circulation effort, and it lasted for a long time. We wanted people to read stories on mushrooms and birds, and we wanted people in groups like the Audubon Society and other environmental groups to be involved. I anticipated that each group would subscribe and distribute copies to their own chapters. Each group, including the Science Center, had their own lists. With this approach we could deliver the magazine in boxes to each group, and the groups could send them to individual members.

I had one volunteer, a good friend, Mickey Isabell, who took care of many details, including delivering the magazines. She was with me for years. Delphine Haley joined me as the writer and editor. She was a good writer, but she had never written anything on her own. She helped edit stories. We did that together. Mickey got them all produced—everything was volunteer then, even the production.

We needed to sell advertising, and that was difficult. I learned that advertisers and businesses were not interested in birds. They do not like a magazine with nature on the cover. *Pacific Search* was not *National Wildlife* or *National Geographic*. *Pacific Search* was all local and regional, and it didn't fly with advertisers.

We sold subscriptions and put on fundraisers. The first fundraiser involved personal experiences, rather than art or objects. We auctioned experiences like a mushroom walk with a world-recognized mycologist from the university. This approach was very popular. We didn't raise a huge amount of money, but we got a lot of interest. It was highly successful, and a lot of people signed up for these events. The prices were not outrageous, but we thought experts and authors would attract people. It was a people experience. Now everybody is doing it this way.

In the early 1960s, we had one woman, Alice Smith, who was the lead editor, and she came every day. She was getting headaches from the cigarette smoke in the office. She told me she could no longer work because of her headaches. I began thinking if cigarette smoke affects the health of one person, why does anybody need to smoke? So I told everybody they could no longer smoke in the office. No one really complained. They didn't like it, but this was the first time anyone suggested that they shouldn't. We instituted a smoke-free building, and they would have to find someplace else to smoke. We had a couple of smokers that did quit their jobs.

Because of these vacancies, I advertised for the position but indicated it was a smoke-free office. I think it was the Seattle PI that wouldn't run the ad because of the no-smoking comment. Now, of course, all offices are smoke free.

Nature doesn't have any humor in it. It is really not funny, so to spruce up the copy, I wanted a few cartoons or jokes or something that would make people laugh at the human condition. I put out a notice that we were interested in some nature-related cartoons. We got a few. It takes a lot to make me laugh or even to get the joke. Someone usually needs to explain it to me. We received jokes that just weren't funny—couldn't get any rise out of me.

I thought it was is hopeless. I wondered if anything would come that could make me laugh. If I can laugh, the world can laugh. There isn't much humor in a story about a mushroom. We sent word around to invite submissions of cartoons or jokes of any sort that would relate to this audience, and initially we didn't get any.

One day a guy walked into the office. He looked a little bit like an owl. Very quiet. He dropped an envelope on my desk and said, "I hear you want some cartoons." I opened the envelope. I just cracked up laughing. There were three cartoons. I knew we needed to publish all of them. They were the first thing I'd seen that made me laugh out loud. I think the cartoons were something about dinosaurs or cows.

The man's name was Gary Larson. I paid him $25 each. Up to then everything written and contributed was volunteer. He didn't ask for money, but I knew I needed to pay this guy something. I wanted them all, and we printed all three. Gary was working in a music store at the time. Later he had cartoons published in the Seattle Times, and then pretty soon he was published all over the world. Now we know him as the author of *The Far Side*.

I never saw him again because he got famous. That was the end of the cartoons sent to the magazine. I never forgot him. He wrote a book later, a kind of a memoir, because he became a wildly successful cartoonist. In the book he wrote about his whole life, and he mentioned that when he first started cartooning he brought three cartoons to a little nonprofit magazine. He was working in a music store at the time, but he always liked to draw. He was amazed that when this little magazine published his cartoons, they even gave him money. It was the first time he had been paid for what he loved to do, and that convinced him he would then draw cartoons. This was the beginning of his career. He quit the music store job and then sent cartoons everywhere. But not to me.

Mickey was good at doing everything; she was a loyal friend. The company had gotten bigger, and I had lots of help. I told Mickey one day that she wasn't needed anymore. She was volunteering, and the work she was doing was done by other people now, and I actually told her that her job at *Pacific Search* was over. I thought she understood what I had told her. She came back the next day and said, "I think you need me. I'm not quitting." How do you let go of a volunteer?

Delphine Haley was our editor and writer. Delphine wrote her first story through my pushing. She had done typing and office work of all sorts before. I was finally able to start paying her. Delphine stayed with me a long time. Alice Smith became another editor.

I hired other people, such as a circulation manager, and then we had to have salespeople. I needed another editor to help Alice, and along came Peter Potterfield. He came to us as a junior editor, and he was full of energy and full of ideas. It was Peter Potterfield who came and said the magazine was never going to make it because could never get sufficient advertising. We couldn't find the advertisers willing to support the kind of advertising I wanted to run.

Pacific Search started in 1963, and I sold it in 1986. For me, it got a little bit boring, and I saw it going in a direction that didn't interest me. It was no longer doing history, which really interested me, but I didn't want to do patio furniture and cooking. The traveling articles were fine, and covering the museums and archeology was fine, since we had wonderful photographs and stories.

Peter was running it in his own way, and I wanted to get out of debt. Peter was aggressive and productive, and he was a good writer and good editor. He ended up being the editor of the magazine. He actually ran the whole operation. Because of Peter's influence, we changed the name from *Pacific Search* to *Pacific Northwest*, to make it sound more regional. Peter gained attention as a finalist for the National Magazine Award for General Excellence as editor of *Pacific Northwest*. Peter has since published numerous books.

After twenty-three years of dealing with the magazine, I found a buyer. It took a while, but I did sell it. At the same time, my sister and I decided to sell KING Broadcasting, inherited from our mother. I had accumulated a big debt over the magazine; I had subsidized it. It never made money. We never sold the right amount of advertising because it was a nature magazine. We did move into more travel and history.

When I sold it, it was an asset sale. A magazine doesn't have anything to sell. The asset was the circulation, which was what the buyer wanted. The sale of the magazine and the broadcasting company got me out of debt, which had escalated, since the bank was charging 22 percent interest. I couldn't even keep up with the interest.

Harriet had a wonderful ability of attracting young, undiscovered talent interested in nature and the natural world. Art Wolfe was one of these unique individuals. Art shared the follow thoughts:

Harriet's story is a story worth telling. She is such a clear-thinking lady. I started with her in the late 1970s, right out of college. I graduated from the University of Washington in 1977. I was an art major, and during the art program, I was really a mountain climber on weekends. During the week I would be studying and painting, but during those college years my allegiance shifted from painting to photography. I loved to be in the mountains and loved the speed at which I could create original compositions. What I learned during the week I applied to my photo compositions.

When I graduated in 1977, I was a substitute art teacher and also spent time introducing myself to Eddie Bauer, North Face, and REI. I ultimately got work up on the walls of these beautiful outdoor stores. At that time, I also started knocking on the doors of publications like *Pacific Search* magazine. That was when I met Harriet, in the late 1970s. I can remember it to this day.

The *Pacific Search* office was on Fairview Avenue. Walking up the stairway into the editorial offices of *Pacific Search*, I met Harriet. She seemed to be open to this young man who approached her about doing some photography. At first, I was struck by how open she was, how friendly she was, and how willing she was to invest in the work of a young person not yet a proven artist. That was what got me started. I think to this day she likes to say that she was my first publisher, and I would not dispute that.

Over the years I did many articles for the *Pacific Search* magazine, which then later became *Pacific Northwest*. I had multiple articles that appeared, and it was the catalyst to go beyond, to go to New York, to go to Washington, DC, to approach editors with *National Geographic* and the *Audubon* magazine.

Another chapter in my life occurred when Harriet exhibited an interest in traveling. Over the years I began taking people on safaris, taking people down to the Antarctic and to Cuba. Harriet and Alex joined me on some of these trips. Harriet brought her entire family on a trip to Antarctica, and it was really cool to see Harriet roll up her sleeves and basically embrace wherever we went. I believe she is of the generation that was not delicate. They had money, but they could just as easily sleep in degraded places, if that were necessary. Over the years I have taken the new rich on trips, who are delicate, who complain at every turn—you wouldn't find that with Harriet. She would just roll up her sleeves, and whatever happens, happens, with no comment or complaint. I just love that about Harriet.

When you look back at the entire Bullitt family, they were very much media people and broadcast people, and who knows who Harriet's mother introduced to the world through the TV stations. Harriet is part of a family, as you know, that was out there doing things, not sitting idly by in a gated community. They were an active part of the community.

Sleeping Lady provided a platform for environmental discussions and groups. I made at least two presentations at Sleeping Lady. (I think one for the Chelan-Douglas Land Trust and one for the national Audubon Board.) I've never heard any negative expression or negative energy coming out of Harriet. That is a part of her marvelous spirit and her longevity. Her spirit is what carries her forward. It is something that I would love to emulate in my own life. I look to Harriet as a role model to emulate in my life.

I admire Harriet that she had a tugboat. This is what makes Harriet so interesting. She is not a normal socialite. I don't see Harriet as a socialite. She can run in the circles of the socialites perfectly well, but she has never been pretentious about that.

Harriet went with me on a trip to Africa with some other friends of mine. We had a great adventure. I think it was in the mid-1990s to a remote park in Tanzania. We went up into the mountains, and there was a fresh water spring, but in the back of your mind you didn't know if there were deadly snakes or if there was a crocodile in the pond, so everybody, including myself, was reluctant to jump in—yet Harriet just took off her clothes, she had a bathing suit already on, and dived in and started swimming around. I thought, "Here are people thirty years her junior or even forty years her junior that are reluctant to do what she is doing," and that is something I focused on over the years. After twenty years, that is a memory I have of Harriet. Diving in that lake without hesitation. That embodies what Harriet Bullitt means to me.

I love the spirit of the woman. I love the fact that you're doing this, Werner. It is an important story—Harriet has been a huge figure in the Northwest. She reminds me a lot of Hazel Wolf. These are special women who were perfect for the Northwest. They weren't pretentious. They filled their lives with energy and interesting people, and what is not to love about that?

Harriet made friends easily, and these friends assisted her in accomplishing many of her ideas. One of her groups of friends was known as the Good Old Women's Network Society (GOWNS). The GOWNS was a social group started by Vim Wright, who assembled a few women she thought were outstanding in their field. It is purely a social group. Though Vim is no longer living, the GOWNS continue to meet. Vim was the director of the Environmental Studies Division at the University of Washington. Estella Leopold, professor of botany at the university, was also involved and continues to be a good friend. Chris Gregoire, who at the time was Washington State's attorney general and later governor, was a member of the group. There were also a couple of legislators or former legislators. Estella has kept the group together after Vim's death. Estella recently invited Chris Gregoire's daughter, also an attorney and, at the time, was a member of the Seattle Port Commission.

Once, Estella brought a group of students from one of her university classes to Sleeping Lady to do restoration work in the meadow and also weed control for fire prevention. They studied and helped deal with invasive weed control and damage from other nonnative plants.

An article in the *Wall Street Journal* on June 21, 1994, titled "Green for Greens—Seattle's Bullitt Sisters Tip Balance of Power in Environmental Wars," gave a good insight into how independent and influential Harriet and her sister Patsy had become in the Northwest.

Dorothy Bullitt, who died in 1989, passed on to her children notions about wealth that play into their environmentalism. "They were taught that having money didn't mean you were better than anyone else," says James Ellis, a Seattle attorney and family friend. "And they were taught to put money back into the community."

The sisters also seem to have inherited a certain Bullitt boldness. Their grandfather golfed and fly-fished and never bowed to his handicap. He taught their mother to swim in Puget Sound by trying a rope around her waist and tossing her from the boat.

The Bullitt's growing green clout rankled a lot of people hereabouts. Like much of the old money in the Northwest, the Bullitt's grew on trees, cultivated by the sisters' one-armed, cigar-smoking timberman grandfather. C.D. Stimson, who later went into real estate and multiplied his fortune. To some of the region's upper crust, the sisters' environmentalism borders on treason.

"A lot of us wondered why they can't just build hospitals like other wealthy people," says a retired timber executive who has known the family for decades. Others denounce the sisters as eccentric meddlers who, being in the manor born, can't relate to the concerns of workers whose livelihoods are threatened by environmental measures.

―――― ⚇ ――――

During the years I lived in Seattle, my children went on to develop their own lives. Scott joined the army and went to Vietnam. He came back OK and, with the GI Bill, went through the university to get a sociology degree, which he never used. He became a Seattle fireman and then an airline pilot. Wenda earned her PhD in psychology and education from Stanford. She had a stellar academic career, though in her early life it didn't help her much. She also spent some time at Harvard.

Another friend of mine in Seattle was Wing Luke. He was a Seattle city councilmen and the first Chinese American to be elected to the city council. People admired him a lot, and he had a great reputation and a lot of friends, and his network was wide. He had a lot to do with the group saving the Pike Street Market. I also belonged to that group.

Wing Luke and his girlfriend, Kay, went on a flight with a friend who had an airplane, and I was invited to go with them. I was tempted, but

I had a date that night with someone I didn't especially like, but I felt obligated to go. I later thought I was saved from a fatal flight, but then I thought, "I wish I would have gone, because I might have been able to talk them out of this fatal return trip because the weather was bad." I don't think they got a good weather report before they headed back to Seattle.

Over the years Harriet experienced numerous relationships ending in divorce or unhappy separations. In the early 1990s, Harriet did discover a relationship that brought much joy and happiness into her life. She had switched from the sport of fencing to flamenco dancing and was attending a flamenco workshop when she unexpectedly met a young Russian, Alex Voronin. Alex was in the United States on a get-acquainted tour and happened to be in the Seattle area. He had already purchased the bus ticket that would take him to Chicago in a couple of days.

Harriet suggested that he return to Seattle after visiting Chicago, and they would take the *Owl*, Harriet's tugboat, to the beautiful San Juan Islands. Harriet was not convinced he would return from Chicago as promised, but Alex showed up right on time, and they made plans for their San Juan trip. When Alex came aboard the *Owl*, he saw only Harriet on the fifty-four-foot wooden tug, and he inquired about the crew. Harriet said it would be a crew of two, and off they went. Alex quickly learned that Harriet was an industrious, loving, compassionate, and talented woman.

Harriet and Alex just celebrated their twentieth wedding anniversary. Alex was not directly involved in the development or operation of Sleeping Lady, but he has been incredibly supportive of the work Harriet has accomplished.

""Alex' on the left, "Harriet" on the right,
"Roki" in the middle. Photo by Ken Trimpe.

CHAPTER 5
Inheritance—Fulfillment of Convictions

———— ∞∞∞ ————

My mother wasn't involved in publishing, just broadcasting. She inherited an office building in downtown Seattle that was built by my grandfather. He had acquired his wealth in logging and the operation of a sawmill. From there, he went into investing in downtown Seattle real estate. In 1928 he built the 1411 Fourth Avenue Building, which went on the National Register of Historic Places in 1991. My mother inherited the 1411 building after her father's death, just at the beginning of the Depression. The building was losing money, but my mother learned the real estate business quickly and got new tenants back in the building, and it started making money. Then she got bored with real estate and got interested in the broadcasting business. She later started a small radio station.

She thought classical music should be in Seattle and started KING FM. She learned about a new technology called television and discovered something called a television license. This was in the mid-1940s, and it was the first TV license in the area. She moved forward with television against all legal advice and that of her peers in broadcasting. Her colleagues thought she would experiment and lose all her money, but she thought having a box with a picture in the corner of the living room would be interesting.

Mother bought the first television broadcasting license west of the Mississippi River. After she purchased the license, the Federal Communications Commission froze issuing additional licenses for a while, so she ended up with a monopoly for a few years. She had a head start before others finally got into television, and she was enthralled with the excitement of TV.

It was nothing like the real estate business. It was a fast-moving, fast-paced business with a whole different language and vocabulary that she had to learn. She thought running a broadcasting business was just like any other business: you do what you want to do with it, which is community service, and at the same time you make money. She did it very well.

But the station needed a call identification. She decided that KING would be good call letters, but someone else was using KING at the time, so she arranged to purchase the identification. She also wanted a good logo, so she called her friend Walt Disney to ask him to draw her a picture for the station. He drew a little guy with the body of a microphone and a mic stand with a little face with a crown on top, and it became KING Mic. The new owners of KING Broadcasting Company did not use the logo, but I've been told they occasionally bring it out on special occasions.

My sister and I decided to sell KING Broadcasting Corporation after we inherited, because it was getting too big for us to operate. We were getting older, and we thought it was too large of an asset to leave anyone as an inheritance. Though it had reached a peak a short time earlier, the market for broadcasting companies was starting to decline. The proceeds that could come to us from the sale could then benefit the Northwest and not dissolve into the federal government.

The sale of KING Broadcasting Corp. gave me resources and time, so I moved over to Leavenworth. When Patsy and I inherited KING Broadcasting, we had very little to do with the day-to day-activity. KING

Broadcasting had a wonderful staff. I was the director, but we were happy with the staff and management. We made the decision to sell it based on some excellent financial advice. Technology had also gone beyond where my sister and I wanted to go.

KING Broadcasting Corp. was such a valuable asset, and my sister and I knew we could not keep the proceeds because it would be too much of a chore. We followed the advice of our attorney, Doug Raff, and set up a charitable trust. That meant putting the money from the sale of the entire company into a charitable trust that we could not spend. We would name beneficiaries instead, which each of us did. I named environmental groups and the music center, and then I set up a foundation where I could use money from this trust. I could also take the yield from the trust on which to live. It allowed me to build Sleeping Lady and the Icicle Broadcasting Company.

My sister and I decided to keep the subsidiary KING FM, because Mother started the station out of her love for classical music. She, of course, wanted to make money with KING FM, but it didn't break even for many years. (It does now.)

It was a labor of love for Mother. She loved classical music and enjoyed playing the piano. She thought a classical music station was a good addition to the Seattle area. It was a rather small station, and played classical music exclusively. It had such a loyal audience, we thought we would be scalped and run out of town if we sold it. To honor our mother and to save our own skin, we bought KING FM out from the sale of KING Broadcasting and then set up a nonprofit to own and operate it. All proceeds supported the arts in Seattle, including the symphony and the opera and the Corporation Council for the Arts. We brought in board members who would represent those organizations. My sister and I would keep KING FM in Seattle and make sure it played classical music for all eternity.

Compared to the sale of the KING Broadcasting Company property,

KING FM was a relatively small percentage of the total, but the organization had to have some kind of surrounding entity. We didn't want to keep KING FM ourselves, so we set up a nonprofit called Beethoven Inc. Beethoven Inc. could own KING FM, which would continue to be for profit, sell advertising, and play classical music, just the way Mother had set it up. We kept KING FM both to honor our mother and because we believed in how she established it in the first place, like how Grandmother had helped start the Seattle Symphony and the Cornish School.

We set up a separate for-profit corporation that had a board of directors. The new corporation would be the owner of KING FM, which was a commercial radio station. (A nonprofit corporation can own a commercial corporation.) Beethoven Inc. was controlled by this board of directors. Patsy masterminded the arrangement, but she didn't trust any of the prominent high-profile city officials who loved classical music. She didn't trust them to protect advertising for a minute. All of them loved to listen to classical music, but they thought advertising was dirt and shouldn't exist.

We knew the station would need to survive on advertising, but we knew there would be differences of opinion. So the corporation was set up so that the majority of directors would have the vote each year, and the ones who didn't have the vote in a particular year would know have a vote the next year, so in that way they took turns. The board included representative from the arts, the symphony, the opera, the ballet, the museum, and the different art institutes in Seattle. None of them knew anything about advertising.

As the board-member term limits came to fruition, the terms were varied so that the next year different members would vote. That way they had every reason to be careful of their votes, since they know next year they wouldn't have one. This system worked so well that when I formed The Icicle Fund Foundation I implemented the same system.

With the sale of KING Broadcasting, we knew there might potentially be a lot of money going to the government, and we didn't want any of this money going to the military. We didn't want to send tax dollars to Washington, DC, to help pay for another war. By turning it into a nonprofit corporation, we knew the money would stay in the Northwest, and it could pay for things we believed in.

Chapter 6
Harriet the Reluctant Developer

<hr>

Sleeping Lady Mountain Retreat materialized because the Catholic Diocese of Yakima needed to divest itself of the Catholic Youth Organization (CYO) property operating in Leavenworth. The CYO camp was across the Icicle River from my home. It shared the border of the property where I spend a lot of my childhood. This property was really my home, and I moved there permanently after we sold the broadcasting company.

I was staying at Coppernotch, and the diocese contacted me about buying the CYO camp. The bishop of the Diocese of Yakima sent a local resident, John Wolf, who I happened to know, to inform me the diocese was wanting to sell the property. They wanted to offer it to me first. It was all downhill from there. I had no ambition to develop a property, but there was no choice but to accept their offer: it would prevent the land from being developed in a way I found unacceptable. This area of the Icicle Canyon at the base of the Icicle Creek was my spiritual home.

Without even thinking, I said yes, without knowing what in the world I would do with it. I didn't want someone else to have it. So, Bishop George, who later became a cardinal, came to Leavenworth. I really admired him, and I made the deal to purchase the property with him. He seemed to be a caring person, and he cared what the community thought about the ownership change. He wanted to keep good relations with the neighborhood.

I loved Father O'Grady, the camp director, and I miss him today. I loved to hear him talk with the kids. While Camp Field was in operation, I would come over once in a while. In my little cabin across the river, I would hear the church bell, and sometimes I would come over, especially on Easter or some special occasion. He welcomed everybody, even if they weren't Catholic; everybody could come for communion. Everybody was welcome in the church.

Father O'Grady told me directly that when he was teaching school in the Yakima diocese, he encouraged his students to question their theology. This approach was not acceptable back then, so he was exiled. They replaced him and sent him someplace where he would be isolated and couldn't do much damage, which turned out to be Leavenworth—the Siberia of the United States. They assigned him to Camp Field, which wasn't doing very well. He looked around at this beautiful valley and thought this was heaven. He immediately organized the camp and attracted youths, and it thrived. Many children who attended are grown today but still remember their experience at Camp Field with Father O'Grady. He transformed Camp Field and he transformed many youths.

Harriet wrote the following account of Father Joe O'Grady and published it under what she labeled "publisher's bias." This beautiful writing is added because it not only shares a great insight into Father Joe O'Grady but also illustrates the wonderful writing style of Harriet as she shares her admiration for Father Joe:

Father Joe: A Maverick Man of the Cloth
In Leavenworth, going to church isn't what it used to be.

Bring me roses in the wintertime…
When they are hard to find.

A handmade banner with these words hangs in a chapel at the foot of Icicle Canyon near Leavenworth, Washington. All fieldstone and wood, the chapel rises from a rocky outcrop beneath towering alpine peaks and overlooks the river gorge. Celebrating mass inside, with a live jazz beat and a children's choir, is the priest of Camp Field, Father Joseph O'Grady, a maverick intellectual who has spanned a cultural chasm in his adopted community and carries the spirit of springtime all year.

At the Easter service this month, one might expect to enter a cloud of soap bubbles, drifting clear up in the vaulted ceiling. The young communicants have bubble pipes and are passing the soap solution around. Or there might be helium balloons: a few escape, bouncing off the ceiling—all a celebration of sheer joy. The congregation will be wearing jeans, shorts, and sneakers. After lively hymns, chants, and Catholic prayers in English, Father Joe will walk down into the congregation to give his sermon, encouraging the children to gather round him. He will weave stories together in a soft, informal voice, leaving a message of hope, memorable to old and young. Everyone who wishes gathers round the altar for communion—not just the Roman Catholics—and embraces during a pause.

Father Joe's thinning white hair and snowy beard give age to a young face and slender build, and the folds of his white robe almost cover the tips of the faded jeans and sneakers beneath. Warm blue eyes show serenity with a fun-loving sparkle. His hands and feet show hard work.

During his seventeen years in the valley, Father Joe has

endeared himself to residents who were suspicious of him when he first came. Some resented him and even abandoned the church because of his liberal practices. "I had to take that risk," he said. Since Leavenworth's pre-1940s roots of mining, railroading, logging, and moonshining, the once free-swinging valley has evolved into a square, fundamentalist Bible Belt. Father Joe entered this scene and did not fit the mold; he never adapted his principles or style to "fit in": he just cared enough to reach out and make a difference.

Born in Lynn, Massachusetts, in 1931, Father Joe attended St. John's Seminary and then moved to Yakima, Washington, where he taught in a Catholic high school until 1966. He incurred the wrath of the archbishop by violating some old-school approaches to teaching, like letting the children ask questions and take initiative in finding answers. This was a diocese where priests were forbidden to read the news or talk in their quarters, where the school bells signaling class changes were considered "the voice of God."

Labeled subversive, Father Joe was then "exiled" to manage a summer camp program on a twenty-acre church-owned wilderness tract outside Leavenworth. The diocese, suffering a large debt, offered no funding. There were some dilapidated camp buildings left from the Civilian Conservation Corp days of the '30s, and there was the beautiful wilderness chapel on the rock—empty.

Instead of despairing, Father Joe surprised the church brass by finding his niche and starting a seventeen-year love affair with the Leavenworth Valley. With neither parish nor church funds, and with the beard, jeans, and demeanor so alien to Leavenworth, he was nicknamed the hippie priest by the townspeople.

Father Joe started out by assuring everyone that he was not going to raise funds in town. Instead he made friends in the bars and over card games, became the confidant and counselor of all who came to him, and presided over marriages, deaths, and births, whatever one's denomination. "I will marry two people as long as they are sure of their commitment to each other. I am not their judge."

With two faithful helpers, Father Joe set about to build and sell a children's camp program and workshop curriculum, which now includes such diverse subjects as marriage encounters, alcoholism, geology, and minister preparedness. How does he make ends meet? "Irish blather," he said, "and sometimes one needs big, sad eyes."

Father Joe has also endeared himself to the business community by bringing at least three thousand retreat guests per year into town to shop and has even served a term as president of the local Rotary.

When I probed some of Father Joe's inner convictions, he warned that "law for its own sake is detrimental to freedom. Literal interpretation of the scriptures is not justified and can lead us astray, to live at half-mast instead of at full throttle. We lose out on the adventure that is meant to be part of life. If you live without law, that doesn't mean that you are lawless. The people who have shown us the greatest avenues of growth did not do so by inventing a series of laws. Now the fundamentalists are very much given to strict interpretation of the law. They're not making any choices of their own. While using portions of the scriptures to back up what they say, they ignore others. For example, the Letters of Paul lists to whom the law should apply: children, and beyond that, only thieves, robbers, murderers, and no-counts. Anybody who has his act together does not need law."

Father Joe recently discovered how many friends he had when he underwent major surgery for cancer. He didn't expect to pull through but credits his returning vitality to the power of the many prayers for him. "My confidence in prayer, if ever in doubt, is completely unshakable now," he said. "I know it works; I can feel its force.

"The most important discipline is to make something of now—to create the gift of the moment. Sometimes it's the gift of the moment. Sometimes it is sweeping the floor, and sometimes it means to swim against the tide, or to be a rock in the middle of the rushing river."

As one friend said, Father Joe "makes the garden where he is." He has brought Icicle Valley roses in the wintertime—a true rarity.

Several of the youth impacted by Father Joe still live in the Leavenworth Valley, though they may no longer belong to the Catholic Church (perhaps resulting from their learned freedom to explore their spirituality). It illustrates the impact Father Joe had on so many young people and the freedom he gave them that urged the children to venture into the unknown. They were always encouraged to take a new look at the gospel and celebrate the spectacular creation that surrounds the Leavenworth Valley.

Bishop George told me the diocese had to sell Camp Field because of financial challenges. The bishop was brought to the diocese because he was a numbers person. He looked at their financial history and said, "We can't do this—it doesn't make any sense." He told me they had many aging priests and nuns, and the church is obligated to take care of them.

The church has homes for these folks, and they need to keep the homes in good shape.

Bishop George was brought in to straighten out the finances in the diocese. The church owned a lot of property, and Camp Field wasn't a profitable property, requiring subsidies. He decided that Camp Field must be sold.

It was a place I would want to protect forever, with the Icicle River running between our respective properties. So the question was what to turn this property into, and that question lead to what Sleeping Lady has become. It took a lot of thought and planning.

Then Werner Janssen came into my life and was able to supervise a lot of the production of the property. It took a lot of time and thought and planning and management to get it to where it is today, where it is growing like an organization of its own.

I wanted to preserve the CYO site from developers who might build condominiums. You never know what someone else is going to do. I really bought the property to prevent someone else from buying it, so I could decide what to do with it rather than letting someone else decide. Around that time, I remember sitting on the hillside with the balsamroot in bloom and thinking, "What in the world could this place look like?" A wildlife refuge didn't make sense. It wasn't big enough to put a fence around it. It needed to be a people place, one that could have a wider influence and draw people for conversation.

It was hard to develop a mission. At Coppernotch, our family lodge, ten or twelve people would get together who had a mission but didn't know how to fulfill it. They would talk about a need or project. "Since we don't have funding, how are we going to raise money?" I would give them a lecture, telling them to stop talking about the money and concentrate on what we needed to do. Too many groups working on restoration talked about the money before they determined their mission. We'd figure out what it cost and how to get the money, but first we had to decide what we wanted to do.

One issue we wanted to address was the return of the salmon. This is still an issue today, though it is more important now than it was then. Many conversations about this took place at Coppernotch, which worked well because we finally concentrated on what we wanted to do. After about three days at Coppernotch, we came up with our written mission. We ended up with a parent group called Save Our Salmon, which later became a major group and received government funding. And all this started in the living room at Coppernotch. Sometimes, groups would come to Coppernotch just as friends to talk about issues based on this experience.

The name Sleeping Lady, the name of the mountain, I first heard when I was a little girl from an archeologist staying at Coppernotch. He looked up at the mountain and said, "There is a sleeping lady." So that's what we always called it. I tried to find out what the Indians around here knew about it, but the only information I gathered was that they had ancestors who were buried in those hills. Father O'Grady might have been embarrassed to cause the young boys to look up there and see a prone woman, so he called it Kamiakin, a chief of the Yakima tribe, but for me the mountain will always be Sleeping Lady.

I had the idea to develop a conference center where we could get people with different ideas together and do the same thing we enjoyed so much at Coppernotch. That idea for Sleeping Lady never changed. We began setting up conferences like the Simplicity Conference. The National Audubon Society board was the first group to register.

The nonprofits and environmental groups don't come as frequently now, but those that do come with groups stop me and tell me that they experienced a change in themselves here. They have been inspired by the natural setting, and they appreciate that we haven't spoiled the area.

When groups ask me to say a greeting, I always tell them about the music center and emphasize that art and music is a part of the life here.

Even during the final construction days, when the chamber music festival occurred, the students would practice out on the decks and under the trees. Some of the young students (who are much older now) occasionally come back and share how well they remember that experience. Even the workmen remember it. Some of the construction workers had never been exposed to classical music, and it impacted their lives. The introduction of music and art was a major part of the anticipated Sleeping Lady experience because music and art are nondestructive human functions.

My mother continued to have an impact on the beginning of Sleeping Lady, not only through Fritz Kreisler's piano. She also loved the *Post* magazine covers and would tear them off the magazines and put them in a box. She told me she had collected these covers in case I wanted them someday. Somehow that box of *Post* covers ended up in Leavenworth. When we were beginning to work on the interiors of the Sleeping Lady, our interior decorator, Josephine Wong, saw the box of covers and immediately saw their value. She insisted that they be mounted and displayed in the Salmon Gallery, the chapel lobby.

The following is a portion of an article titled "Profile," published by *Meetings in the West* in January 1997. The Sleeping Lady operation began in July 1995.

Profile of Harriet Bullitt

Business Philosophy:
    To maintain profitability and long-term quality service to our constituency and the community without compromising either one. To focus on the identity of the place, which is ecotourism, in a setting where groups can enjoy

nature, good food, outdoor recreation, and music, along with good conferencing services.

Best business decision:
    Selling my interest in two Seattle businesses, allowing me to retire debt free and to build Sleeping Lady.

Worst business decision:
    Investing in a movie.

Mentor:
    My mother.

Person most admired:
    The Dalai Lama, for absolute serenity and his ability to communicate it.

Competitor you most admire:
    I've looked for competitors and haven't found any yet for this place.

If you had to choose another career:
    To be a better parent.

Favorite movie:
    Babette's Feast.

Favorite vacation spot:
    The Canadian Gulf Islands on our tugboat.

CHAPTER 7
Development Team Begins Its Work

THE REMAINDER OF THE BOOK will not be, for the most part, transcriptions of actual conversations with Harriet, but to a greater degree, shared memories of the development team of Harriet Bullitt, Reed Carlson, and Werner Janssen as they worked together to bring the ideas Harriet developed for Sleeping Lady Mountain Retreat into reality.

Initially, Harriet was advised to work with an engineering and development firm, who came in and intended to do the site layout and building design. They would also arrange for all the contractors to complete the project. This approach wasn't acceptable to Harriet. They assumed that she would be involved in terms of paying the bills but not be involved in any of the other decisions. Harriet was uncomfortable with this approach. She began looking for a firm that would be open to her vision and value her thoughts and opinions, one that would design a site that would live up to her dreams as well as meet the sensitivities of the environment.

Harriet selected Jones and Jones Architects, landscape architects and planners from Seattle, Washington. Jones and Jones had a stellar reputation for environmentally sensitive work. It had a worldwide reputation for its work developing zoos with exceptional sensitivity to the care of animals and the environment. Johnpaul Jones, a partner at Jones and

Jones, was the principal architect for the project. His Native American heritage also brought a special insight into the sensitivity of dealing with the earth and the environment. This was important to Harriet.

The following was written by Johnpaul Jones sharing his thoughts about working with Harriet as principal architect for the project:

I remember clearly the first time I met Harriet. It was at the Jones and Jones studio in 1990.

We were contacted by C3MG, a consultant to Jones and Jones. We had been recommended to Harriet as architects and planners for the master plan and design project called Sleeping Lady at Icicle Canyon, southwest of Leavenworth, Washington. Harriet's representative arranged a meeting to discuss her project at the Jones and Jones studio in Pioneer Square in Seattle.

We were so excited to be considered for her project. We prepared a couple of things we thought would be interesting to Harriet to help her select an architect for the Sleeping Lady project. We did not get a chance ahead of time to visit the existing church summer camp facility she wanted to remodel. However, a friend gave us some photos of the existing site that helped us prepare for the meeting with Harriet.

When Harriet appeared at the Jones and Jones studio for the interview, I was taken back by her open, honest look, and how beautiful she was at an elderly age! She was so open to discussions about our past work and how our design and planning related to what we thought she wanted accomplish at Sleeping Lady. She was very quiet and smiled a lot at our presentation.

Harriet particularly enjoyed the wall of architectural images we had pinned up for her to look at—photo images of National Park Service park facilities and other wonderful mountain facilities we had designed. She enjoyed discussing the wall of images.

I thought I had done a good job understanding her goals and vision for Sleeping Lady during the interview, and as she left the studio, she gave me a wonderful smile that broke down any worry or concern I might have harbored. As she left, I noticed that she was wearing Levi's and a simple outback top. I thought to myself, "I would like to work with someone like this."

I found out later that immediately after Harriet left the Jones and Jones studio interview, she went directly to a coffee shop to discuss the Jones and Jones presentation with her advisor. She loved what she heard and saw. I'm glad Harriet selected Jones and Jones. I have enjoyed working closely with Harriet over the years.

The beginning of the master plan process was interesting, to say the least. As the Jones and Jones team began investigating the old summer camp facility, buildings, and site landscaping, I sat in on a couple of utility meetings with Harriet's selected engineer team while they discussed important site utility items. I was fascinated by the engineer team's focus on what they called a "cave" project—an outdoor amphitheater facility for the future Sleeping Lady grounds. I wasn't aware of this proposal until I sat in on the meeting. I looked across the meeting room at Harriet, who had her eyes closed. It looked like she was asleep. I found this odd, since the engineering team was talking about spending a lot of Harriet's money to accomplish this project. An amphitheater facility to seat a four- to five-hundred-person audience with a stage and other support theater spaces felt unrealistic to me. Something seemed odd and wrong.

After the meeting I asked Harriet if my wife and I could come over to her family compound over the weekend, spend two nights, build some fires in the fireplace, cook some food together, and just have an informal discussion about what her vision and goals were for the entire Sleeping Lady project. She agreed and arranged for the weekend.

As we prepped food for cooking and shared warm fires and dish duty over the weekend, I learned from Harriet what she really wanted to accomplish at Sleeping Lady. It was not to do a cave amphitheater but to keep things simple, honest, and sustainable, and most of all to create a place where many different groups could come together to solve community, social, and environmental problems—a lovely, natural place with big trees, meadows, a river, and countless beautiful mountain views.

The next week Harriet removed the previously selected engineering team, and together we began to create Sleeping Lady as you see it now. Many people have helped create Sleeping Lady, but it was Harriet's own personal vision and goal that laid the foundation for what has followed.

When I was a young boy, I was told that I was dyslexic and poor at reading and spelling. To this day I still struggle with this. However, over the years practicing architecture design with many different clients, I've come to realize that there are many folks with drawing dyslexia. As Harriet and her newly selected Sleeping Lady team began the formation of the project, and as the Jones and Jones team developed design options, our goal was to show Harriet creative ways to design each facility. I noticed in the presentations that Harriet she listened intently to what we said and smiled. She responded when she thought she liked one of the present-ed options. I realized I needed to give her some pointers on how to "read" design drawings so she could make a totally informed choice rather than only listen to what we said. I coached her on how to read them, and over a few months she became quite good at understanding the drawings, and as a working team, we moved forward.

The Sleeping Lady project was built by a number of ex-cellent construction contractors and subcontractors over the years. From my many years in design and construction, I've found that if the owner or their representative walks onto the construction site the construction team often stops them to discuss some current construction issues. Often the contrac-tor's suggestions are excellent; however, often they are not. How this relates to Harriet is as follows:

On one of the many construction site visits, to check on construction progress and quality of work, we found many changes to the architecture and site work that differed from the designs, which often made things difficult. Once I looked into who had given the OK to make the contractor changes, and it turned out to be Harriet. When Harriet walked across the construction site each day to get to her home across the river, many construction folks would approach her and ask many questions. The construction folks took her smile and soft words as an approval of their suggestions.

So, I had to sit down with Harriet and ask her to not discuss the project with the construction folks and tell them to ask the architect. She was surprised. We discussed what she could say to contractors so they would not take her smile and kind words as an OK to make changes. It worked. She did not have to stop crossing the construction site each day, and she could continue to be friendly with the various construction folks.

I spent twelve years working with Harriet and her Sleeping Lady team: it was a good experience! One thing I came to understand, from the beginning in 1990 to twelve years later, is that Harriet is a unique person. She has a strong personality and has great enthusiasm for doing the right thing, and she remains a special friend.

As the planning work continued with Jones and Jones Architects, Harriet decided she would set up her own development team, including herself as an active team member, rather than hiring another outside development and construction company.

Reed Carlson had done numerous construction projects for Harriet both in Seattle and Leavenworth. She contacted Reed to see if he would join her for the Sleeping Lady project. Reed was a photographer who gained experience in carpentry skills in his young life, including a time as a volunteer at Holden Village after college. He also worked for the Forest Service and was involved with Peg and Bill Stark on their project gathering artists, photographers, and writers together to support and encourage locals interested in creative ventures. The group known as the Extended Family met in Harriet's chalet on the south side of Icicle Creek, just across from the Camp Field property. At that time, the Chalet was not in good shape, but it was usable.

Reed suggested that she contact me to join the development team. I had been manager of Holden Village when Reed was one of the volunteers, and I was now living in Leavenworth. I met with Harriet at Coppernotch for an initial conversation. This visit-interview was the first time I met Harriet.

I did come close to meeting Harriet one winter when she participated in a cross-country ski race at the golf course. I had volunteered to help as one of the timers for the event. As I recall, Harriet came in last, but finishing the race in her sixties indicated to me that she was a very special person with determination and a matchless joy in celebrating life.

Shortly after our meeting, Harriet asked me to join her development team with the responsibility of bringing her concept for Sleeping Lady Mountain Retreat at the former Camp Field facility into reality.

I actually began working for Harriet as a contracted team member in the fall of 1993 and became an employee of Sleeping Lady Construction on January 1, 1994. We spent several months in preparation and planning, specifically beginning to contact and hire contractors to accomplish the variety of construction work needed in this extensive project.

Camp Field, the CYO camp, was still rented out for several events when Harriet purchased the property, and she wanted to respect those agreements to the greatest extent possible. The Camp Field chef and the dining room were still functional, and Harriet would have dinners in the dining room for friends and associates during the initial months of her ownership. These early months were also spent working with the neighbors on Icicle Road, acquainting them with the project. We responded to questions and concerns they expressed as to traffic, potential operational noise, and the type of activities that would take place once the Sleeping Lady Mountain Retreat Project construction phase was complete and the operation was initiated. Johnpaul and the Jones and Jones team made several trips to the project site, with maps and drawings of the proposed layout of the project indicating how existing Camp Field buildings would be saved and reused, emphasizing that they would maintain the natural setting. Although there were some in the area who expressed serious concern over the extent of the project, Harriet and the Jones and Jones team did an excellent job of patiently working with the neighbors and gradually bringing the vast majority to understand this project would have minimal impact on life in the surrounding area.

When Harriet, Reed and I initially met as the development team,

Harriet had several very specific nonnegotiable requirements for the project:

- No trees would be removed from the existing landscape.
- All the existing Camp Field buildings would be utilized or moved to accommodate the new site plan.
- The maximum amount of recycled material would be used in the new construction.
- Only contractors who agreed to protect the environmental integrity of the site would be hired.
- All contractors would agree to recycling all discarded materials either through reuse or by helping to return discarded materials to be used by other projects in the area.
- All contractors involved would be local, from the greater Wenatchee Valley, to the greatest extent possible.
- Building supplies would be purchased locally, to the greatest extent possible.
- No discarded materials would be deposited in the county landfill. (This requirement was dropped after it became apparent that it was not practical for this extensive project.)

Harriet was aware of the rumors circulating in the valley that claimed she would be coming in to accomplish this extensive project and would be bringing in contractors from the "west side," instead of giving locals a chance to participate. But Harriet loved both the valley and the people in it and wanted their participation to the greatest extent possible. She communicated in every way possible that it was her intent to use local workers and contractors.

It was very evident that Harriet was not interested in a more typical management style for the project. She was more interested in friendship and conversation and sharing ideas. I don't recall that we ever had a formal management team meeting, but I do remember numerous conversations while enjoying a cup of tea or coffee or taking a walk around the construction site, especially on sunny days. Getting a feel for the site was critical as we finalized the plans.

It was also evident that her concern for the environment and establishing an example of how environmentally conscious development can be done was more critical than keeping costs to a minimum. Harriet even requested that, before any site plan had final approval, members of the Jones and Jones team would do a visual survey of how deer and birds enjoyed the site. After all, these critters were the honest residents of this portion of the valley along Icicle Creek. Perhaps some of this approach came from the Native American influence of Johnpaul, but this was also true to Harriet. The fact that the Sleeping Lady Mountain Retreat's healing properties has had such an influence on so many guests very likely comes from the fact that Harriet, the reluctant developer, was concerned for nature. She insisted that the development's disturbance would be minimized. Each day's work was initiated with an attitude of a certain admission of embarrassment and a request for forgiveness that nature was being altered and, in some cases, destroyed.

As the development began, a small group of Harriet's friends gathered on the property just north of the new registration office to participate in a Native American ceremony acknowledging the changes and disturbances that would soon take place. The following is the text of an article appearing in *The Wenatchee World* on April 17, 1994, written by publisher Wilfred R. Woods.

Harriet Bullitt's Sleeping Lady Retreat Center renovation project got under way officially Friday afternoon. It wasn't your usual groundbreaking affair, although a shovel was finally used.

This was a Native American dedication, complete with two Medicine Lodge members from Tacoma who performed incense smoke and pipe ceremonies with the dozen and a half of us present.

The retreat center construction will be no ordinary affair. Jones and Jones Architects from Seattle have instruction from Harriet that there will be a minimum of discarding of materials, and a maximum effort to blend the remodeling into the land.

Jacque Martinson (Many Moonbeads) and Margo Dietrich (Medicine Bear) brought the grasses and herbs and tobacco which, set alight in an abalone shell, were wafted over each of us. And the pipe ceremony had each of us pass the pipe around the circle in turn, as prayers were said.

The work has already started on some of the old buildings being jacked up, ready to move by the Bates movers from Wenatchee.

Fifteen buildings will be moved and 15 new ones built to take care of a total of 180 people when complete.

Some of them are the old Civilian Conservation Corp buildings, but they will be rebuilt with four "pods" of four buildings each, with thirty-eight people housed in each pod, plus other housing as well.

The former Camp Field chapel will be rebuilt with a three-thousand-square-foot lobby with dressing rooms and restrooms included. The remodeled chapel will hold about two hundred.

There will also be a new dining room next to the Icicle River.

Johnpaul Jones of the architectural firm is a Native American of Cherokee and Choctaw descent. He described to the group the care with which his firm will supervise the construction of the new Sleeping Lady center.

As Harriet Bullitt said, "We want to add beauty here, not destroy it."

Helping supervise the construction are Reed Carlson, who has worked for Harriet for many years, and Werner Janssen, who joined the staff last year.

Harriet Bullitt was assisted in wielding the shovel for the groundbreaking by her husband, Russian-born Alexander Voronin.

Construction of the new center will take twelve to fifteen months to complete.

———— ⚇ ————

When Harriet Bullitt met architect Johnpaul Jones, she sensed that they spoke the same language and a partnership was born. Much of his dedication to and inspiration for the Sleeping Lady project was his spiritual feeling for the site inspired by his Indian heritage. "The site is a living thing," Johnpaul said. "We need architecture to recede and nature to come forward. We need to listen to what the land is telling us."

Johnpaul Jones wrote the following which he titled, "We Are Connected":

Sleeping Lady is more than a retreat and conference facility. It is connected to something larger than those human activities. It is connected to what we share across our diversities. It is not a vision or a philosophy of life. It is not a path of enlightenment. It's something much more understandable. It was sent by our ancestors to help us know that we are connected to something larger than ourselves. Art often expresses this connectedness.

There is a large black canoe sculpture at the Canadian

Embassy in Washington, DC, by Haida Indian artist Bill Reid. This black canoe is filled with animals, spirits, humans, and plant forms. The canoe is totally full. There is hardly any room in the canoe: it is full of wolf and wolf tails, cedar hats, and human paddlers, beaver paddlers and bear spirits hanging on to humans, who are part animal spirit.

The canoe's message is about connectedness. It conveys a message visually. There is no interpretive text. It is not important to understand every detail and the significance of everything about the canoe sculpture. It is more meaningful to be transported by its message—what ones sees and feels.

This is what visitors to Sleeping Lady relate to and carry away with them. They feel connected to something larger than themselves.

Early in the process, Wilfred Woods introduced me to Scott Hosfeld. Wilfred had participated in the Bach Festival in Chelan, and he thought there should be a place here for music, and not just in the summer. He brought Scott over, thinking this was a venue where Scott could perform year around. Some of the thought started with the chapel. I knew it wasn't going to be a church, and Father O'Grady was gone. Running a church wasn't in my qualifications, and so the Camp Field chapel needed to be a theater. The Catholic diocese in Yakima came and decommissioned the chapel, removing the altar and the communion ware. We were able to keep the candlesticks, but they took everything else that was church-related. Removing the altar officially decommissioned the structure as a church.

Scott, Marsha (his wife at the time), and I visited the Banff Centre for Arts in Alberta, Canada, to see what this very successful music center had accomplished. We wanted to learn from their successes and avoid their mistakes as we developed the Icicle Creek Music Center. Scott was trying to persuade me to build all these small individual practice rooms, which was a good idea. Scott had much bigger ideas and hoped I would create something that might duplicate the Banff Centre for Arts and Creativity.

From the beginning, music, art, good food, and the celebration of nature were the foundation of what I wanted to do with the Camp Field site. I wanted to provide inspiration to go out and change the world. The development of the Icicle Creek Music Center, initially a part of Sleeping Lady Retreat Center, was an important part of my dream.

Emphasis on a music center featuring both instruction and performance was not part of the Sleeping Lady development when it was initially envisioned. The influence of Wilfred Woods, along with his friendship with Scott and Marsha Hosfeld and my love of music, added the determination to expand the development to include music and eventually art and theater. None of the initial site plans or architectural drawings included a music center, but that changed quickly after the meeting with Wilfred.

The piano I have today, in my new home above Kingfisher Dining Room, is the same piano that was in the house where I was born and grew up and took piano lessons as a young girl. I practiced all my lessons and studies on that piano. It was a major living room piece in our house in the Highlands.

Several months after the construction actually began, the entire project almost came to a sudden end. On July 24, 1994, the Rat Creek fire began a couple of miles west of Sleeping Lady in the Icicle Valley. It was midafternoon on the twenty-fourth; the sound of fire trucks began moving up the valley with sirens wailing. In a short time, the twin-rotor helicopter began dipping water out of Icicle Creek just below Sleeping Lady and in front of Harriet's home.

The Chelan County deputy sheriff soon appeared in the construction office and notified us that everyone would need to evacuate immediately. The fire was burning up the slope, across the Icicle Creek, and behind Harriet's home. The construction site was full of piles of very dry cedar roof shingles removed from the buildings. The entire site was covered with dry wood and partially dismantled buildings. If glowing embers were to land on the site, the facility would disappear. The entire mountain slope to the south of Sleeping Lady and immediately behind Harriet's home burned all night with its self-generated windstorm. Viewing the fire from several miles away, it appeared as if there was no chance the construction site had survived.

Harriet related, "The next morning when I came home, I headed to the Chalet to see if it had burned. The house was OK. The fire crews were not able to park a fire truck at the Chalet because there was no alternate escape route, but the Columbia Helicopter #42 dropped several buckets of water on the Chalet to wet it down and save the historic structure." The fire had not touched the construction site, allowing the project to continue, but construction activity was delayed for two weeks as the smoke cleared and the air quality improved.

CHAPTER 8
Construction Begins

———— ∞ ————

HARRIET WROTE THE FOLLOWING PROJECT mission statement as it relates to the philosophy of the development and operation of Sleeping Lady:

> Sleeping Lady, a meeting and networking center, will be developed as a profitable operation with facilities for conferencing and recreation for people seeking harmony with nature.
>
> Planning will seek to preserve or enhance the health-giving properties of the landscape, foster a sense of contact with nature, and provide an atmosphere of solitude, quiet, and slow tempo. Opportunity to enjoy and participate in the arts will be part of this mandate.
>
> Its design will permit the highest possible degree of energy efficiency and water conservation, within limits of financial feasibility, that others may replicate. Recycled building materials will be used where possible; new materials will be selected with consideration of the energy required to produce them. Special attention will be given to noise producers like heating plants and vehicles. Energy efficiency and quiet operation should go together. Features that do not add to

safety, comfort, good dining, and enjoyment of the arts, or that detract from experiencing the feel of the setting will be minimized if not avoided.

Project business rationale—develop a facility and operation based on the following premise:

- Environmentally sensitive in philosophy and practice
- Going beyond the surface details to create an ecological example
- Using approaches and operation procedures that are transferable
- Allowing the environmental convictions to be financially feasible
- Thinking in terms of what is most productive, healthy, and energizing, and then what is most efficient.

From the concept phase through design, construction, and operation, the driving force has been working to accomplish an outcome that will provide a meeting experience and an operation viability blending the ideal with the practical.

The design and construction techniques were based on environmental sensitivity, along with the creation of an ambiance providing a physical and experiential situation, fostering meetings and networking in an atmosphere that stimulated creativity and cooperation.

Our theory was that the productivity at meetings is greatly increased when participants feel a level of comfort in their surroundings, valued with quality meals and staffed with individuals who honestly value each guest. When the mind is refreshed with art, music, and architecture, individuals are freed from competitive demands and are able to create a community of cooperation that moves progress and enjoyment to the next level.

The physical size (sixty-seven acres) and its occupancy capacity (fifty-nine rooms) allow multiple small conferences and group meetings to share the space, but the economics allow corporate groups to have exclusive use of the site if privacy or security is desired.

Everyone entering the site detects the commitment to a conviction. Historical significance and the community energy of the past operation were preserved to the greatest extent possible. Preserving the eighteen existing buildings, relocating the structures, and rebuilding them to the latest standards increased the overall cost by 5 percent. The determination to preserve all trees and design and construct buildings around existing trees increased the costs by 1.5 percent, but it resulted in a new facility that had the feel of being in a natural setting with sixty years of natural history.

Birds and animals did not leave the site during construction because the contractors agreed to respect nature as the real inhabitant. Natural landscaping was used to enhance the setting in the foothills of the Cascade mountain crest. The landscaping was also chosen to reduce water consumption and minimize or eliminate chemicals, pesticides, and insecticides. The forty acres of the site requiring landscape maintenance uses no fertilizers, pesticides, or herbicides, and requires 35 percent less water to maintain.

Water features on the site were developed to enhance the diversity of habitat as well as birds and animals. Art features such as fountains and waterfalls use irrigation water, which is then recycled back into irrigating the landscape, so as not to use extra treated or potable water.

A certified organic garden was developed to provide a percentage of produce for the food service and flowers to enhance the visual joy of the facilities. The garden is considered a part of the landscape and provides an additional enjoyment for short hikes on the site.

Significant works of art have been added to the site and primarily to the outdoors. Music is a definite feature of the site, and a music academy is being added to the operation, not only to encourage opportunities for musicians, but also to enhance the auditory delight of the site. Sleeping Lady was developed to provide a holistic experience to participants of meetings as well as the casual visitor. Art, music, architecture, and honest respect for all people create an ambiance ensuring successful meetings, enthusiastic people, and a high return rate for meetings and groups. Even with this emphasis for environmental consideration, the determination to insist on quality, the emersion into art and music, and an operational philosophy of quality over efficiency, Sleeping Lady has reached its goal of profitability within five years.

It is clear that Harriet, in relatively short time, guided the concept of a site plan, a facility, and an operational plan to provide a unique center promoting gatherings that enhance the improvement of society by providing access to nature, music, and art. If you can enjoy this ambiance, even for a brief time, ideas and solutions will flow that will lead to positive changes for all people. This was the dream that Harriet experienced at Coppernotch, and this is what she wanted to provide on a larger scale at Sleeping Lady Mountain Retreat.

Some of Harriet's convictions for the design came from her mother's experiences and later her own in the broadcast business, which was definitely a man's world. At important meetings, men would gather in one of the large suites or sleeping rooms to share drinks, smoke cigars, and make broadcasting decisions. Harriet decided that people should be forced to walk outside in between meetings, as they travel from their housing units to the dining hall and to their meeting spaces. For an effective meeting, participants need to get outside and breathe fresh air and enjoy the aroma of the fertile earth. Harriet insisted on maximizing the window area so you felt like you were outside, rather than the windowless prison that is often offered by many high-rise hotels.

There would be no smoking, not only in the buildings but also on the entire sixty-seven acres of the Sleeping Lady property.

The rooms would be small but comfortable. People should not sit in their rooms to socialize with others. Meeting participants should meet in public spaces, so everyone has the opportunity to join in the conversation. Most of the important discussion at many meetings is in the social hours or informal moments rather than within the formal meeting.

The rooms would not have television, and there would be no mini-bars. Initially, the decision was made not to have air conditioning in the sleeping and meeting rooms, but air conditioning was added later. As soon as it became available, high-speed internet was added to the sleeping and meeting rooms, as well.

Harriet wanted to accomplish this development in her own way, with care and concern for nature. Harriet decided not to hire one major construction company to accomplish the work. She was concerned that a construction company would come in and clear the site of all trees and old buildings before initiating the construction. Harriet was not a "normal construction" person. Professional construction companies are generally given a cost limitation and need to accomplish the work with the greatest efficiency and at the least cost to maximize their profits. Cost was always a consideration for Harriet, but in many cases, it was a secondary consideration compared to environmental sensitivity and emotional interaction between the human feeling and the physical impact of the structures and the natural surroundings.

This was a very unusual project, and it is why Harriet chose to establish her own management and development team, since a professionally trained construction and development team may find it difficult to adapt to this unique development philosophy. The entire project was self-financed. The banks were never involved. Harriet's attorney maintained the legality of the project. Her accountant advised and sometimes expressed valid concerns relating to the escalating costs, but it was Harriet who determined the direction and quality of the project. Harriet always made the final decision.

Through the work and direction of the development team and though the environmental knowledge and sensitivity of principal architect Johnpaul Jones, Harriet's dream became a reality. Awards and recognition were not a priority for Harriet, but because of her convictions and determination, awards and recognition were received nonetheless.

During the early years of the operation the following three Washington State and National awards were received.

April 1997—the American Hotel and Motel Association Enviro-Management Award: Sleeping Lady Mountain Retreat was recognized as an "outstanding example of environmentally sensitive planning, design, construction, and operation." This was presented to Werner Janssen, general manager of Sleeping Lady Mountain Retreat, at the national meeting of the American Hotel and Motel Association in Washington, DC. The award was presented by Senator Robert Dole.

April 2001—American Institute of Architects, Top Ten Green Projects: In recognition of Earth Day 2001, the American Institute of Architects selected ten built architectural design solutions to profile. Sleeping Lady Mountain Retreat was one of the ten facilities acknowledged for the use of green construction material, improvement of indoor air quality, reuse of existing structures, energy and water conservation, and low-impact site development, all of which reduce environmental impact and make a positive community contribution.

September 2001—Washington State Governor's Pollution Prevention Award: Sleeping Lady Mountain Retreat was one of nine businesses and two government facilities recognized for preventing pollution and using business practices that are sustainable, which means successfully meeting the needs of business without jeopardizing the ability of future generations to meet their own needs. This award was presented to Harriet Bullitt and Werner Janssen at the state capitol in Olympia, Washington, by Governor Gary Locke.

A partial list of specific points that developed as the result of the convictions for environmental sensitivity requested by Harriet are as follows:

- Recycled cellulose insulation was used in all the buildings. The insulation is from recycled cardboard, computer paper, and in some of the later buildings from recycled paper from gypsum board. This produces a very efficient and tight building envelope.
- Air to air and liquid to air heat exchangers were used in many of the buildings to recover previously heated or cooled air.
- Low-emission argon-filled windows were used throughout all the facilities.
- Compact fluorescent lighting was used to the greatest extent possible. Path lights also used compact fluorescent bulbs, gradually converting to LED bulbs to further reduce energy consumption.
- Heat pumps were used to provide hot water for the laundry and food service, with heat collectors over heat-producing equipment such as dryers, dish washers, and ice machines.
- Buildings added in 2002 were fitted with geothermal or ground source heat pumps for cooling, heating, and pre-

heating domestic hot water.

- Forty of the 59 sleeping rooms were converted to geothermal or ground source heat pumps to reduce energy consumption.
- The swimming pool and hot pool were retrofitted with ground source heat pumps to heat the pool; propane use was reduced by 80 percent.
- Naturally cold irrigation water was used, but not consumed, to cool or precool a portion of the buildings. The cold irrigation water (fifty-two degrees) was pumped through a heat exchanger and then returned to the irrigation ditch.
- Buildings were located and oriented to minimize the heat build-up and provide natural cooling during the summer months.
- Two Green Mountain Technologies in-vessel composters were used to compost 85 percent of the organic material produced in our food service. This provided a rich supplement for the certified organic garden while, at the same time eliminating six to eight yards of waste material per month normally disposed of in the landfill.
- Cardboard, office and computer paper, and aluminum were recycled.
- Glass that cannot be recycled was crushed in the glass crusher and used for either drainage material or path surface material, with the fine sand from the crusher used to sand paths in the winter, decreasing the problems with ice and compacted snow.
- The pool used an ozone generator supplemented with bromine to disinfect the water. No chlorine was used.
- Linen on the beds was pure cotton, without bleach or formaldehyde.

- No wall-to-wall carpets were used to minimize off-gassing in the rooms and reduce dust accumulation in consideration for allergies.
- All wood surfaces in the interior of all facilities were sealed with water-based materials to reduce off-gassing of petroleum products.

To the greatest extent possible, products for our food service were selected with environmental consideration. An example of this is the coffee, which is shade grown and produced by fair-trade growers.

No construction manual was available to provide directions for establishing this type of project. Sleeping Lady Construction hired its own on-site crew to deal with the day-to-day work of recycling and improving efficiency within the project, which involved multiple contractors. All the individuals hired for the Sleeping Lady Construction crew were local women and men.

The site plan and general building design was completed in early January 1994. The set of plans, including studies on engineering, environmental impact, traffic, drainage, sewage disposal, and water distribution, was submitted to the Chelan County Building Department. Over fifty pounds of plans and studies were delivered to the department. At that time, it was the most extensive set of plans they had ever received.

Most of the contractors hired were nonunion. Two of the major contractors, responsible for the construction of Kingfisher Dining Hall and the Chapel Theater, along with the framing contractor for the housing units, were union. It was necessary to include in the written agreement with the union contractors to agree to work side by side with nonunion labor, assuring everyone would agree to support and value each other's input. It was my observation that all the contractors recognized the uniqueness of the project and the opportunity to create a once-in-a-lifetime facility. They valued the loving and compassionate kindness of Harriet

Bullitt, who was more interested in nature and the quality of work than in speed of the project. It was obvious that Harriet valued the craftsmen, and the workers knew they had a friend in Harriet. She frequently visited the site and always enjoyed conversations with the construction crews.

Sleeping Lady purchased some of its own construction equipment. When the Caterpillar loader was delivered to the site, the regional sales manager arrived with the delivery. He was thrilled to meet Harriet and, on a whim, asked if she wanted to drive this rather large piece of equipment, probably thinking she would be intimidated with the suggestion. He didn't know that Harriet piloted her own ocean tugboat. She didn't hesitate. After a brief orientation, she drove the loader down the road.

The construction of the Sleeping Lady facility was unique in many ways, but perhaps the most interesting aspect of the project was Harriet's insistence the that buildings previously associated with Camp Field must be saved and used in the new project. Harriet had strong feelings concerning history, and she almost hesitated changing what had been Camp Field. Father O'Grady had developed this special place for youth, many of whom were struggling with their own faith. Father O'Grady also struggled with his faith and found a unique opportunity to help youth reevaluate their own understanding of church dogma and rules and to discover the joy of considering God and nature in a new way. Harriet wanted to retain some of Camp Field's healing history and its life-enhancing ambiance in the new facility.

The chapel was the jewel of Camp Field. It was the worship space for the Catholic camp but also served as a concert hall for Camp Field and other organizations in the Leavenworth Valley. The chapel was beautiful but had some functional deficiencies that needed addressing. The chapel had no effective heating system, and the entry was too small.

Harriet knew she would not be using it as a chapel for worship, but she definitely wanted a concert venue. Jones and Jones Architects designed a new entry wrapping around the front of the chapel, large enough to accommodate receptions and even provide additional space for meetings. The beautiful rock fireplace would be retained, along with the entry stairs leading into the chapel itself. The new chapel entry space was named the Salmon Gallery. There was a concern that the Salmon Gallery interior would be too massive and that something would be needed to break up the interior space. Harriet contacted the artist, Dale Chihuly, and discussed the possibility of having one of his expansive hanging glass sculptures to enhance the space. As the Salmon Gallery construction progressed, it became clear that the architectural design was beautiful and complete on its own. The possibility of a Chihuly creation would be considered for another location.

The original rock work on the chapel had been created by a rock mason from Wenatchee, Cecil Lee. His son Mickey was sixteen at the time and got his start as a stone mason working with his father. As it turned out, Mickey's son would now work with him on the rock work in the chapel's remodeling. In addition to the chapel, Mickey Lee did most of the work on the rock walls and also the waterfall at O'Grady's Pantry. Mickey was one of many artists involved in the construction work developing Sleeping Lady Mountain Retreat.

When Harriet purchased the property, there were eighteen buildings. Approximately ten of the buildings were left from the Civilian Conservation Corp days. The CCC was in operation in 1937, listed as Company 6436, and assigned to the Forest Service. Camp Field added additional units, especially the beautiful chapel. Fourteen of the 18 existing buildings would be moved to new locations to fit the new site plan.

Bates House Moving from Wenatchee was hired to move the buildings, with the stipulation that no trees would be removed or damaged during the move. Two of the buildings were actually cut into sections to accomplish the move without tree damage. Don Bates was another of the many artists involved in the project. Bates House Moving did a masterful job, and they were on the site over a six-month period to accomplish the rearrangement of the buildings. Moving the buildings also included establishing the first building for the development of the Icicle Creek Music Center west of the irrigation ditch.

One of the changes in the final planning stages regarded the main access to the site. The original entrance road, Peters Street, was legally a Chelan County road. The architects initially proposed a new access road off Icicle Road, approximately half the distance from the existing entrance to the Meadow Stage. The road would have come through the meadow to the area of the existing parking space. Part of the reason for this proposal was to provide a maintenance entrance separate from the guest entrance. This new entrance proposal was eliminated because of excessive costs.

Chelan County requested Peters Street be vacated to eliminate the county's obligation for maintenance and snow removal, but Harriet did not agree with this request. The county did retain ownership but did agree to officially change the name of the street from Peters Street to O'Grady's Street.

The Camp Field registration office and a portion of Father O'Grady's apartment was moved to the entrance and designated as the gatehouse. This building was then remodeled and became the KOHO 101 FM radio studio. After the radio station was relocated to Wenatchee. the studio was remodeled again becoming the Aspen Leaf Day Spa. The Camp Field dining room was relocated to the entrance and was initially used as the vehicle garage. In recent years, the vehicle garage became the exercise room and was then remodeled again to become the Sleeping Lady Mercantile.

Remodeling of buildings and functional changes began almost immediately as the operation initiated. It was a learning experience, and Harriet had no hesitation changing building functions as the team gained experience. For example, the area originally reserved for crafts was rather quickly remodeled into the Grotto Bar. Since conferences and meetings were the function of Sleeping Lady, it became evident that those attending meetings also needed a place to socialize in the evening.

Construction recycling was one of the important requirements for the project. In 1994, the practice of construction recycling was just starting on a national level. The Sleeping Lady Construction crew had an employee whose main function was to work with the contractors to make sure all construction debris were separated, assuring all recyclable material would be salvaged and not sent to the landfill.

A commercial eight-foot tub grinder was purchased, allowing all wood and plaster board to be pulverized. The material was then used as an additive to the soil in the meadow and various landscaping projects on the site.

The recycling program used at Sleeping Lady was recognized as a leader in the Northwest. It was estimated that approximately five thousand cubic yards of waste was recycled rather than added to the Chelan County landfill. In 1994, the summer edition of the publication *Environmental Achievement* featured the Sleeping Lady project in an article titled "Sleeping Lady Project Could Wake Up Construction Industry to New Levels of Environmental Responsibility."

Minimizing construction pollution was also emphasized. Absorbent mats were required under all construction equipment when idle to eliminate oil contamination of the ground. Fences were put around trees in the areas immediately surrounded by construction to eliminate damage. It was the first time these various construction crews were involved with recycling, but there was great cooperation. Site cleanliness was emphasized, including proper disposal of lunch debris to minimize rodent activity. Construction crews valued Harriet's convictions and did all they could to cooperate, even though it was not a part of their normal routine.

A rather extensive search was conducted for recycled materials that could be used in the various construction projects. In 1994, the State of Washington was supporting an organization called the Clean Washington Center. This organization put together a great list of various recycled materials available in the Northwest. We used this document extensively to make contacts with companies or individuals who were producing recycled products. Unfortunately, a high percentage of the products available were those utilizing recycled tires or made in very small quantities. We did attempt to use recycled wood from dismantled buildings, but several firms in the Northwest specializing in recycled wood did not stock large quantities. They would take an order, then dismantle a building and cut the dimensioned lumber requested, but it might take six months to a year to supply what was needed.

We did look into an interesting product produced in Oregon: wall board made from wheat straw. It had a wonderful natural look. The operation involved one innovative farmer, but when we contacted him, he had only one four-by-eight-foot sheet of wall board available. No more wall board could be produced until after the next harvest.

Recycled fir flooring cut from salvaged beams was used in the majority of the original construction. By 1998, recycled fir flooring was impossible to find, and then later in the project it became too expensive.

The recycled product that we used most extensively on the site was Trex decking. The site design used extensive decking to tie the various clusters of buildings together. The architects had called for cedar decking, but the ongoing maintenance cost involved with cedar was a major concern. We would not consider using cedar unless it could come from a sustained yield forest.

Trex was a relatively new product produced from recycled materials, and at that time it was not used extensively in the Northwest. It was manufactured in the East from recycled plastic grocery bags and hardwood chips from local furniture factories. There were very few large projects using Trex at the time, but we discovered Atlantic City was beginning to use Trex on their boardwalks. We contacted Atlantic City about their experience and received very positive recommendations. That gave us the confidence we needed to use this recycled material. We determined that we would need thirty thousand lineal feet of Trex decking. This quantity was not available in the Northwest.; it was ordered and shipped in two rail cars from the factory.

We decided Sleeping Lady Construction would purchase most, if not all, of the equipment and materials involved in the construction projects. Contractors have a normal markup of at least 10 percent if they order and front the cost for supplies, equipment, and materials. It was estimated that at least $500,000 was saved on the entire project using this approach.

Sleeping Lady was not within the geographical area that would allow the development to connect to the Leavenworth city sewage system. This was potentially a major problem. Because of the size of the project, the initial engineering proposal called for a treatment plant at a cost of over $1 million. A treatment plant would require a full-time licensed operator and much increased maintenance and operating expenditures. It was not financially an option.

Johnpaul introduced us to Dave Ray, a soil engineer and a very innovative designer of septic systems. Dave immediately understood Harriet needed a unique system that would enhance the environment, minimize energy consumption, function with minimum problems, and be financially reasonable to install. Dave was an independent contractor but the State of Washington frequently used his services to solve commercial septic systems and drain field challenges. He was highly respected by the Washington State Health Department, which was a bonus.

Because of the size of the project, the sewage system was under the jurisdiction of the State of Washington Department of Health rather than Chelan County, as would normally occur. This was fortunate since Dave already had a positive relationship with the state. Although it was not a requirement, we agreed to work with the state health department to monitor our operation and provide actual water use and flow figures for the septic system of the hospitality facilities. For the first time, the State of Washington would have actual recorded data from actual measurements. Harriet valued science and research highly and was delighted that an increasing portion of the Sleeping Lady project would provide data measurements and enhance environmental considerations.

In the original design, it was specified that mechanical air conditioning would not be used in any of the buildings. The buildings were well shaded by trees, and all windows would be easily operable for good ventilation. After several years of hosting conferences, however, participants made it clear that air conditioning was crucial for the enjoyment of meeting and sleeping spaces. We began by air conditioning the meeting rooms with conventional units.

Later, air conditioning in the sleeping rooms used a more efficient system known as ground source heat pumps (GSHPs). This system provides very efficient heating and cooling of the rooms and would also preheat the domestic hot water system, especially when the time of year required artificial cooling. The GSHP system uses the mass of the soil, which has a steady year around temperature of about fifty-eight degrees at a soil depth of six feet. According to the Environmental Protection Agency, GSHPs are the most energy-efficient, environmentally clean, and cost-effective space conditioning systems available.

The only option we had was a closed-loop system that utilized a circuit of sealed pipes to exchange heat with the ground. The pipe itself is high-density polyethylene plastic with an expected service life of fifty to seventy-five years. A small pump circulates a mixture of water and non-toxic antifreeze through the pipe. This building-to-earth loop exchanges heat with the surrounding soil and provides the ideal temperature of fluid for the operation of the heat pump. Approximately eight hundred feet of pipe was buried in the meadow at a depth of six feet. This system was yet another example of Harriet's interest in using the most efficient system with the least negative impact on the environment.

Using technology to enhance the environmental integrity of the Sleeping Lady project was important. Enhancing communications to the site was a major challenge. When the operation began in 1995, the only communication access we had was the regular copper wire telephone system used by GTE Corporation in this area. Conferences were beginning to use video conferencing for presentations, and the data speed and capacity of the dial-up option we could offer was inadequate. In 1997, the Washington State Technology Alliance Association held their state conference at Sleeping Lady. Bill Gates Sr. was the founder and president of the Technology Alliance Association, and the conference wanted to use the opportunity to showcase the use of high-speed data transfer. When they realized Sleeping Lady didn't have high-speed capabilities, Gates made a call to the president of GTE, and within a week Sleeping Lady had an Integrated Services Digital Network (ISDN) line, which had not be available at any location in the Leavenworth Valley at the time. An ISDN line would provide Sleeping Lady the fastest data transmission available. At the conclusion of the conference, I contacted GTE and arranged for Sleeping Lady to retain access to the ISDN line. Within two years the system was upgraded to a T1 line. The Technology Alliance Association had a wonderful conference, displaying all the technology they needed, and Sleeping Lady ended up with high-speed data technology. Fiber optics was just becoming available, but the T1 line provided the capacity and the speed needed.

The ISDN line gave Sleeping Lady and the Icicle Creek Music Center the capability of having the first live broadcast of an Icicle Creek Music Center Chamber Music Festival concert. We worked with KING FM to broadcast the final afternoon summer festival concert that season.

In 2001, we decided to install fiber optics to all the main buildings, providing high-speed data through the T1 access to the conference rooms for meetings and conferences. We also extended fiber optics to the music center once it was constructed. This provided internet access as well as a fire detection system connection. Later, the Canyon Wren concert hall and the Meadow Stage were added to the fiber optic system, giving broadcast capabilities to these concert venues.

———— ⚬⚬⚬ ————

Harriet definitely wanted water features on the site, especially a swimming pool for family and registered guests. Icicle Creek flowed along the south border of the property, and Harriet loved to swim in the river as she had enjoyed from childhood. There is no doubt that Harriet's first choice for a swimming feature would be a swimming hole in Icicle Creek. The legality and liability of this was questionable, though, and there was only a portion of the year when Icicle Creek could be used for swimming, as it originates in the glaciers and snow fields not far from Sleeping Lady. The water temperatures are not ideal for swimming the vast majority of the year.

Harriet did not want a rectangular Olympic-size pool but rather a pool that would be constructed out of a rock formation to provide the feel of a mountain river pool. An outcropping of bedrock was located on-site, but as often happens with nature, it was not an ideal location or size to allow an entire pool to be blasted out of the existing bedrock. Artificial rock had to be incorporated into the natural bedrock to complete the design.

The State of Washington required approval for all commercial pool designs. The state had seldom, or perhaps never, been approached to consider a commercial design that was not a rectangular pool with very standard decks and a smooth bottom. The final approval was received only after extensive negotiations. Construction of the pool continued and was near completion before the final approval came through. Harriet did not want to use chlorine in the pool, and Chelan County eventually approved our use of an ozone generator but required us to use bromine with ozone to meet their requirements.

There were also requests for a hot therapy pool along with the swimming pool. It turned out that if we called it a "hot pool" rather than a "therapy pool," along with eliminating the air jets and benches normally included in a therapy pool, it was much easier to get our plans approved. The entire State of Washington had one person reviewing the design and installation of commercial pools. The inspector told us they would prefer our pool to be rectangular with a standard pool bottom. They wanted the pool deck to be uniformly the same distance above the water and as smooth as possible to eliminate any standing water. Those requirements did not fit Harriet's strong desire for the natural appearance of a pool on a mountain rock outcropping.

We were able to successfully negotiate with the state to have our rock pool. The equipment building for the pool's various pumps and water filters was designed with a grass roof, to eliminate a visible metal roof. Every effort was made to have the pool experience duplicate a swim in a mountain pool, though a normal mountain pool would not have a security fence around it. The state didn't allow much compromise on this, but with the slope of the ground it was possible to minimize the visual impact of a fence from within the pool.

The use of artificial sculptured rock was a work of art, but it also increased the cost of construction and future maintenance. A young artist specializing in sculptured rock was brought in specifically for the pool project. The company Natural Creations, Casey Castillo with his six-person crew, was on the site over a six-month period. Their primary work was with the swimming pool, but they also accomplished an important portion of the interior of the Grotto Bar.

To create sculptured rock that would fit the specific look of the Icicle Creek area, Casey went up the Icicle Valley and made latex fiberglass molds from actual boulders he found that fit our purpose. No damage was done to the original boulders. Once the molds were available, they were used to make concrete rocks that, when painted, matched the natural rock. No seams were visible between the sculptured and natural rock. He even used dental tools to match the lines and fissures in the natural rock. Casey had previously worked on projects for Bill Gates, Paul Allen, and Ken Griffey, and he joined the many other artists who enhanced the development of Sleeping Lady Mountain Retreat.

During the summer and fall of 2003, information began to circulate that Cashmere Mountain was under consideration for an underground national laboratory. A *Seattle Times* staff article published November 5, 2003, indicated that University of Washington physicist Dr. Wick Haxton was one member of a group investigating the best possible site for the lab. The proposed lab would conduct research in physics, astrophysics, earth science, and geomicrobiology, studying particles form the sun, the formation of minerals and hydrology in the earth, and microbial life deep underground.

Dr. Haxton contacted Harriet to inform her of the proposal and also to determine Harriet's feelings, as she was an important member of various environmental groups in the Northwest and the owner of Sleeping Lady, located just a few miles from the proposed laboratory site. Harriet loves science and research and was intrigued with this proposal.

Dr. Haxton held at least one meeting at Sleeping Lady to present information to the public and answer questions from those living in the immediate area. Harriet initially opposed the project but then expressed a more positive attitude after meeting with Dr. Haxton. The *Seattle Times* article quoted Harriet saying, "The Icicle Valley is a sacred place, but it's not pristine anymore. It's a grab bag for developers."

As more information became available concerning the construction process (specifically the number of trucks driving down Icicle Road and East Leavenworth Road to remove the drilled rock from the tunnel), the negative impacts of the project became evident, and Harriet had a change of heart. Harriet joined the majority of people in the Leavenworth Valley in opposition of the project. For a variety of reasons, Cashmere Mountain was not selected for the project.

The Icicle Canyon continues to be threatened by development. The number of people who love to hike, camp, and climb often crowd the canyon. For example, the water coming out of the canyon is critical for irrigation, for Leavenworth city water, and even for the future of the Leavenworth National Fish Hatchery. Fortunately, with various groups working to safeguard the beauty and environmental integrity of the area, more and more of the canyon is being preserved.

Harriet has always appreciated the sacred nature of Icicle Canyon, from childhood horseback riding through the canyon to the emotional feeling of its spiritual ambiance. She has now, for a lifetime, worked to preserve this wonderous place.

Chapter 9
Art and Nature

———⊶⊷———

Harriet made it clear from the beginning of the Sleeping Lady project that art and music would be a vital element woven into the final design and operation. This reflected her love of art and music instilled by her mother during her youth. Harriet was not a "collector" of art but rather an "encourager" and "discoverer" of art and emerging artists. The amazing Harriet and her magazine *Pacific Search* introduced new artists to the Northwest and the world.

The following passage is from the great artist Tony Angell in October 2015:

> I first met Harriet through her magazine *Pacific Search*. It was around 1967. Harriet was the editor and publisher of the magazine, had established a cadre of science writers and photographers who brought a contemporary focus to the natural history of the Pacific Northwest. Every current subject, anthropology through zoology, was photographed and written about by local leaders in these fields. (Ivan Doig cut some of his earlier writer's teeth publishing matters on local history in the magazine as well).
>
> If you had an interest in the human and wild nature of

the Pacific Northwest, *Pacific Search* was your go-to publication. This handsome publication was only fifty cents, and always dramatically illustrated with well-researched articles—the content was diverse. A May 1971 issue, for example, provided information on building a saltwater aquarium and, a few pages further, included a summary of pollution-free geothermal power.

I offered Harriet the use of some of my drawings and short essays on birds of prey, in hopes that they might be included in her publication. With some editing and fine tuning, she put me in print for the first time. As it turned out, the magazine that included my images and ideas became, for me, the first part of my passage into this world of art and writing.

I was in my twenties, and I recall there was an informality in our writers' meetings that assembled in the old Bullitt house, which was still part of the KING Broadcasting Company property. Harriet's mother, the venerable Dorothy Bullitt, would often stroll through, offering an idea in her "basso profundo" voice about the events of the day, which we would all acknowledge. I'd bring in drawings with a short, typed manuscript, and the following month there it would be, reaching out to readers throughout the Northwest.

These were the years immediately after the Century 21 and Seattle World's Fair. There was much cultural momentum, something of a Renaissance for Seattle as Pioneer Square was being renovated and restored, and the arts were really on the boil with galleries opening up regularly. One of them, the Richard White Gallery, was among the most respected, and on the encouragement from Harriet and others, I took my work there for consideration of a showing.

I well remember that little place at the top of the stairs at 311 ½ Occidental Avenue. The tiny gallery was indeed the "half" of its address. I went in down the long hallway, my meager portfolio in hand, and there at the end of the room was Dick White, sitting at his desk, having a glass of gin at 11:00 a.m. A short conversation ensued. "What do you want?" he asked. "I want a show!" said I. "What do you have?" he continued. "Drawings," I say.

He asks for a look-see, and after showing him a few I had done for *Pacific Search* he says, "Wait a minute. I know you. You have your drawings in *Pacific Search*. I love them." And there you have it. Thanks to Harriet and her magazine, over a half century ago, my art career was launched locally in the gallery I remain with today, now called Foster/White.

Along with my artistic and writing pursuits, I was also involved in environmental education for Washington State. Harriet often provided her time and expertise participating in a number of teacher education programs. She became an active member of our Advisory Council for Environmental Education and would often travel to Olympia to attend meetings when we had them there. When our office hosted a panel of civic and business leaders to discuss the environment, Harriet never failed to participate. She had this authoritative yet disarming manner of presenting arguments that directly addressed the point, whether it was an argument for more efficient use of energy and other resources or preserving an exceptional part of our natural heritage here in the Northwest.

This period of time included our office participation with some of the national leaders in raising important environment issues including Paul Ehrlich (*The Population Bomb*), Francis Moore Lappé (*Diet of a Small Planet*), Barry Commoner, and

Jacque Cousteau. Harriet participated in supporting their educational efforts with her participation on panels and by providing contributions to the teacher education programs. Barry Commoner impressed her with his outspoken efforts to influence the Nixon administration to make better policy decisions regarding the environment. Harriet even provided a hefty contribution in support of Commoner's run for president in 1980.

KING Broadcasting, under the leadership of Harriet, Patsy, and Dorothy Bullitt, was singular in giving special emphasis to matters of the environment here in the Pacific Northwest. Harriet assembled focus groups that included civic and governmental leaders to talk about the important issues of the day. Under the directorship of Ancil Payne and with the likes of newsmen Bob Simmons et al., the important social and environmental concerns and events of the day were kept before the public. I am convinced KING Broadcasting, with Harriet at the helm, made a significant difference in how and what the public was able to perceive and eventually make decisions on regarding the environmental destiny of the state.

When Harriet set out to convert the former campground alongside the Icicle Creek in Leavenworth into a world-class retreat center, she had further honed her interests and knowledge on matters of our natural heritage here in the Pacific Northwest. Her time spent on the Board of the Nature Conservancy allowed her to provide information to the staff and other members of the board as to what distinctive natural areas existed east of the Cascade Range. She did so as she was also investing her time, energy, and resources in opening up opportunities to the larger public to come to Sleeping Lady to savor and understand the vast and complex benefits of experiencing life amid the environments there.

Harriet also saw the importance of integrating art into the Sleeping Lady experience. Indeed, the collection of works by sculptors in glass and metal that occupy the grounds are among the most powerful public art pieces relating to nature to be found anywhere in the Northwest. That I should have the opportunity to have some of my creations as part of this collection is an honor I will always cherish. I well remember when I sat down to share my idea for a "greeting" sculpture with Harriet as we sat on the ground at Sleeping Lady. I envisioned a pair of bronze ravens (a common visitor to the woods along the Icicle River) that, placed near the entry to Sleeping Lady, would serve as emissaries for the visitors who would come here. I told her of my experiences with these birds, who would sometimes approach me in the wilderness and suggest to me that they were representative of all the diverse wildlife I might discover there. Rather than challenging me, I felt the birds conveyed a welcoming spirit, inviting me to come into nature to discover and learn the endless wisdom that resides there. Harriet's response to my proposal was perhaps all of two minutes before she said simply, "Let's do it!"

The powerful commitment Harriet has applied to her belief in the arts was uniquely demonstrated when, in 2001, she directed her energies and resources to the development and fulfillment of the Watershed Art Project. Harriet wrote an opening section of the publication that was produced by the project. She eloquently summarized the importance of sustaining the stewarding of the Wenatchee River and supported the local team of three artists, Gretchen Daiber, Cynthia Neely, and Gretchen Rohde, that made it happen. Over the course of the artists' visits and stays in the region, many paintings, sculptures, weavings, and photographs were produced. The result is a magnificent artistic tribute to the watershed that, over the course of public showing, articles, and eventually a permanent collection, builds a lasting bridge of aesthetic appreciation and information about nature.

The architecture itself is an expression of art as well as function. Johnpaul was well aware of this emphasis; it was one reason that we chose Jones and Jones Architects to do the architectural design. Harriet felt strongly that artwork should be within nature and not exclusively displayed inside the buildings. Her love of nature also dictated the night lighting on the paths and in buildings. Night lighting should be minimized so everyone could enjoy the night sky to the greatest extent possible. Johnpaul and his crew visited the site several times, walking the paths after 10 p.m. with lighting samples that were used to determine what level of illumination would be acceptable to Harriet. The path lighting was specifically designed to maximize the enjoyment of the night skies.

The rock walls created by Mickey Lee, around the Kingfisher Dining Room, the entrance to the registration office, and at O'Grady's Pantry were not only functional but were also the location for rock carvings. Rock walls helped with the flow of traffic but also provided seating spaces, creating inviting opportunities for conversations within nature and sharing the space with the art.

Harriet commissioned Gretchen Daiber, a local artist, to create a series of rock carvings. The first sculpture utilized two granite rocks originally located at the entrance to the arrival area for vehicles. One sculpture was a coyote and the other a weasel. The coyote and the weasel are positioned to give the appearance that they are cautiously observing each other. The unique carvings required the entire carving process to be done on-site, with the rocks in their final location. Guests and staff were able to enjoy observing Gretchen's creative process. Her on-site work took a little longer, since many people were observing and asking questions and enjoying conversing with Gretchen as she worked.

Gretchen was commissioned to do additional sculptures and now has at least seven rock pieces on the Sleeping Lady site. A coho salmon welcomes people as they unload and approach the office. The river otter watches people enter the Kingfisher Dining Room. The raven keeps an eye on the activities in the beer garden. A mountain pika, perched on the rock wall, welcomes the people as they enter the Grotto Bar. An owl sits on the mantel at O'Grady's Pantry and enjoys the conversation around the fireplace. (The fireplace at O'Grady's was the creation of rock mason and artist Mickey Lee.)

Bob Anderson, another local artist, was at the time on a Sleeping Lady construction crew. Harriet loved art, and the artist's level of fame was not significant to her. Bob was living in the area at the time, and his real passion was woodcarving. Like many artists, Bob had a day job and happened to be working with one of the many contractors at Sleeping Lady.

Bob had carved a beautiful, life sized, spotted owl five years earlier. For one year the carving was on display at the main Eddie Bauer store in downtown Seattle. For a time, there was an environmental controversy involving the spotted owl, so Bob put the piece in his attic, for fear damage or destruction by the public. Logging in Washington State was major business, and saving the spotted owl had become a highly emotional issue.

I encouraged Bob to bring the owl carving and show it to Harriet. She immediately offered to purchase the carving and put it on display on the main floor of the Salmon Gallery. The carving was so lifelike that some assumed it to be stuffed rather than carved from wood. After completing his work at Sleeping Lady, Bob moved to Montana, devoting himself to his carving full time, specifically birds and other creatures in nature.

Gene Drake from Cave Junction, Oregon, carved the *Returning Salmon* sculpture. It began as a two-thousand-pound chunk of soap stone; when the sculpture was complete it weighed twelve hundred pounds and portrayed seven salmon dancing their way upstream to spawn. The completed and polished soap stone provides the appearance of scales on the salmon. Gene confessed that until he began to polish the soap stone, he was not aware of its specific texture.

He offered to deliver the sculpture in his old panel truck, and I inquired about insuring it beforehand. Gene made it clear that, until it was in place, it was his responsibility. If the sculpture were damaged in transport, he would merely make a new one.

The Salmon Gallery had its name before the salmon sculpture was in place. Plans were made during the construction process to set a sizable granite boulder in the entrance of the gallery as a base for the sculpture yet to be delivered. The boulder was shipped from Marenakos Rock Center in Issaquah, Washington. To accommodate the sculpture, a slice of rock needed to be cut to the proper size of the sculpture's base. This granite boulder was lowered in place before the roof of the Salmon Gallery was installed.

Randy Betz, another local artist, created exquisite wood projects utilizing timbers and logs. Harriet commissioned Randy to make the Viking Table, sized specifically for the Hearth Room in Kingfisher Dining Hall, with an emphasis on recycled materials: the timbers were obtained from a local dismantled fruit warehouse, and its surface is two old beams notched and spliced together. The beams retain the original bolt holes, right on the table's surface. It is fifteen feet long and its total weight is fifteen hundred pounds. Randy was also commissioned to fabricate and install the tamarack log sections against the north wall of the Salmon Gallery.

In 2000, an outdoor stage venue for larger outdoor concerts was requested, and we built in the meadow. Jones and Jones Architects designed a beautiful stage structure utilizing peeled poles as the main architectural feature. Randy was again commissioned to create the log portion of the stage. Several poles came from Harriet's property at Coppernotch, and Trex recycled material was used for the stage decking.

When construction began on the Icicle Creek Music Center, three log bridges were needed to provide access across the irrigation ditch to various sections of the music center site. Randy was also commissioned to fabricate and install these log bridges.

Randy was an artist, but at Sleeping Lady most of his work was also functional, contributing to the day-to-day work and operation as well as creating ambiance and an appreciation for the natural.

Richard Beyer was a well-known and a greatly loved artist in the Northwest. *The Art People Love*, a book written by his wife, Margaret Beyer, shares his work and his life. One of his most famous sculptures, *People Waiting for the Interurban*, is located in the Fremont District in Seattle. People enjoy standing by the figures or even dressing them in hats and gloves for the winter season, and many like sitting or snuggling with others.

Harriet commissioned Richard to do two sculptures. One, a woman releasing a salmon into a stream, sits at the entrance to the organic garden. The woman is fashioned from bronze and the salmon from cast aluminum.

The second sculpture is a humorous tongue-in-cheek nine-foot salmon walking on his tail fins and carrying a five-foot, six-inch man in a fishing net. The entire piece is cast aluminum and was poured in two separate molds, one casting for the salmon and the other for the man. Richard had a specific vision for the location for the sculpture. He wanted it in a small grove of trees and facing the sleeping lady's ridge in the mountains, on his way to a party. The sculpture is located at the north end of the meadow pond.

Tom Jay was one of the Watershed Art participants. He was the artist and creator of the *Salmon Bell*. Tom completed the clay sculpture for the bell on his pedestal outside the Nuthatch meeting room and took approximately a year to complete the casting. It was initially displayed at Miller Gallery in Leavenworth at the opening of the Watershed Art show. After the show, it was transported to Sleeping Lady and hung from a mounting designed by Jones and Jones Architects and fabricated by Randy Betz. The mounting was designed to support the heavy bell without need to create a structure that would require soil excavation.

The most ambitious art installation was by Dale Chihuly. Chihuly was first contacted in 1994 when Harriet thought the Salmon Gallery might need some enhancement. The Chihuly project was put on hold for a time but still in the works for some space on the Sleeping Lady site.

The day after Thanksgiving, 1996, Harriet received a call from Chihuly that he was on his way over to discuss an idea he had, and he wanted Harriet to review his idea for a possible project. As we sat in the dining hall, Chihuly sketched some initial thoughts on a napkin, even writing down some of the crew who he thought could provide leadership for the project. The napkin remains in my files to this day.

Chihuly proposed doing a glass sculpture, permanently mounted outside. He guaranteed the project would be complete for unveiling by the end of December that year. This would be his first-ever permanently mounted outdoor glass sculpture.

A flurry of activity began in the next few days, as coordination was critical for the completion of the thirty-day project. The proposed sculpture would have a series of handblown glass icicles mounted on a stainless-steel armature. Chihuly's crew did research on sealant or caulking for the small opening in the end of each handblown icicle. Sample icicles were tested in a flash freezer and a wind tunnel to check their integrity below freezing and in winds up to forty miles an hour.

A consulting geologist from the University of Washington was hired to inspect the granite boulder chosen for mounting the sculpture. The plan was to drill a hole eight inches in diameter into the boulder, then secure a six-inch stainless-steel pipe into the hole. It was critical not to compromise the boulder's structural integrity or destroy it. We found an adhesive that would not expand during curing so the boulder wouldn't fracture in the process.

Chihuly reported that, once Harriet approved the concept, he assigned virtually his entire crew of thirty people to work twenty-four hours a day to produce the glass icicles and set up the installation for final inspection. By December 10, over one thousand handblown icicles ranging in length from twelve to thirty-six inches were complete, including attached stainless-steel, allowing each glass icicle to be individually fastened to the stainless-steel armature. The entire sculpture was assembled in Chihuly's warehouse in Ballard for one final inspection and approval by Harriet.

On December 15, a semitruck backed up to the Salmon Gallery and unloaded fifty-four boxes of material containing the entire sculpture. Chihuly hired Tiedeman Construction, a major contractor already working on the site, to fabricate a platform around the boulder for efficient installation. When it began to snow on the second day of installation, a clear plastic cover was installed over the work area, allowing the setup to continue. On December 21, the crew of ten artists and technicians arrived from the Chihuly studio in Seattle to accomplish the sculpture's final assembly.

Chihuly decided on one change to the design: a heating cable would be attached to the stainless-steel frame. This would serve two purposes: to melt some of the snow as it accumulated during a storm (and thus reduce the snow load on the glass icicles) and to have real icicles form on the bottom of the glass icicles from the melting and refreezing of the melting snow. Unfortunately, the snow loads did not present a problem, and real icicles did not form from melting snow, so the heating cable was disconnected.

Chihuly had two teams of photographers document the installation process. Chihuly documents a select number of his installations in books detailing the concept and installation of a particular artwork. The completed book outlining the work on the Sleeping Lady sculpture was published a year after the installation: *Icicles: The Icicle Creek Chandelier*.

The unveiling of the sculpture was scheduled for December 28. Chihuly chartered a bus to bring the fabrication and installation crew from his studio. By the night of December 29, a major snowstorm hit, closing both passes for the next seven days. The snowstorm provided an immediate test of the sculpture in terms of major snow loads. No damage occurred.

The first permanently mounted outdoor Chihuly glass sculpture attracts the attention of those staying at Sleeping Lady as well as the many who drive in just to see the Chihuly glass sculpture.

In 1998, we decided to increase the housing capacity of Sleeping Lady, resulting in another major art creation and installation. The new housing cluster did not have any advantageous natural tree shade, so Harriet decided to add a water feature to provide a physiological cooling effect along with air conditioning.

Harriet knew exactly which artist could accomplish her concept— Jerry Tsutakawa, a Northwest artist carrying on the tradition of his father, George. Harriet's mother had commissioned George to create the impressive indoor water sculpture in the new KING Broadcasting Building.

Jerry submitted a sketch of a courtyard water feature and fountain for what was then referred to as the Fountain Cluster.

Harriet wanted to develop a water feature without waste, and did not want to use treated or potable water, because of environmental considerations. We worked with Jerry and developed a design to utilize water from the irrigation ditch, but purge the fountain several times a day and return the purged water to the pond, eliminating the need to treat the water. The pond water was then used for irrigating the organic garden. A concrete vault was installed to the west of the Fountain Cluster and placed underground to eliminate the pump noise that could disturb the surrounding area.

Jerry was a delight to work with. His family often accompanied him on visits to Sleeping Lady. Jerry's mother was with us the day the bronze sculpture was lowered onto the fountain pool's mounting bolts. She had previously accompanied her husband George on many of his installations; it was definitely a family experience.

The piece was dedicated as the *Freedom Fountain*. The Kairos Quartet from the Icicle Creek Music Center provided some formality to the occasion. Many participants, including Harriet, removed their shoes and waded in the pool as part of the dedication ceremony.

The extensive art displays found throughout the Sleeping Lady property provide a delightful emotional surprise when you see them. The art at Sleeping Lady is not confined to a garden or gallery but rather displayed around the site, easily enjoyed from the many paths. Some of the art, especially the rock carvings by Gretchen Daiber, are very subtle, and people often miss them the first time they pass. Their purpose is to enhance the experience of celebrating nature.

The art is not intended to dominate or provide a substitute for nature; rather, the art enhances the enjoyment of nature itself. Art lifts the spirit of all who observe as they walk between meetings or to Kingfisher Dining Hall. Spirits full of awe and wonder are more conducive to creativity in meetings or in celebrating relationships or in the pure enjoyment of honoring each day. Harriet's love of art might have originated through her mother's influence, but it is also a part of Sleeping Lady for her own emotional well-being. Harriet knows that what brings joy into her life also brings happiness to the many others who visit.

CHAPTER 10
Concluding the Beginning

—⊷⊶—

SLEEPING LADY MOUNTAIN RETREAT WAS initially designed as a conference center with the intent of attracting meetings and conferences to help solve societal and environmental challenges. With Harriet's experience at Coppernotch, she knew that significant changes can occur after gathering people together and providing an atmosphere in nature with good food and meeting facilities encouraging conversation and discussion. To stay true to this, Harriet initially requested that Sleeping Lady should keep weddings to a minimum. Financially it was necessary to encourage nonconference business, but in the early years, conferences had priority.

In addition to art, music, and nature, quality food was high on the list of priorities for Harriet. Word circulated in the culinary field that Harriet was looking for a chef to develop and organize a quality food service for Sleeping Lady. Damian Browne, originally from Australia, was working in Seattle and was intrigued with what he heard about this new conference center in Leavenworth. Damian shared the following:

> I answered an advertisement to fill a chef's position for Sleeping Lady, a new conference center, in a year-round mountain setting. Looking back, it was a bit of a gamble. The concept for Sleeping Lady was definitely "right brain,"

and pretty dodgy for most logical thinkers. It lacked most of the amenities typical in other conference resorts. It quickly established itself as a leading conference facility and a favorite with environmental, educational, and self-improvement groups wanting to facilitate real change in a setting designed specifically for that purpose.

As it was explained to me during the interview, the food was to be on the healthier side, largely drawing from the organic garden on-site. Being health conscientious myself, it sounded like the perfect gig. After years of working in Seattle-area hotels, I had had enough of working in basements opening boxes upon boxes of frozen chicken breasts and repeating the same generic food service night after night. I was ready to reacquaint myself with real food, and this mountain setting and slow-food concept was the perfect place to do it.

Harriet was instrumental in the planning of the food service concept. Everything was designed to encourage a more relaxed and casual dining experience where the barriers of pretense were replaced by fostering communal hospitality. The food was to be served camp-style, which was to encourage conversation between people standing in line and so guests could interact with the cooks. The dining room tables were mainly large rounds to stimulate good conversation; the food quality was elevated to compensate for the camp-service image. Money that could have been spent on waiters in tuxedos was spent on offering better-quality food choices. I loved pretty much everything about the vision and spent the next eleven years trying to stay true to that plan.

The creating of Sleeping Lady was an exciting time. As a part of a hotel company, I had experience with many hotel openings, and they always require more work than you can ever imagine. Still, Harriet's vision to create something like Sleeping Lady stirred a dedication from many, and I'm sure much of their passion still lives among the wood and nails, the plates and cutlery, the linen and pillows.

The Icicle Creek Music Center was in development at the same time as Sleeping Lady. Housing, concerts, and practice rooms were all at Sleeping Lady. The Summer Chamber Music Festival was always scheduled in July, and it was a magical experience.

During the first years of the music festival, construction was still in progress. Frequently, musicians would be practicing outside to the sound of power saws and pounding hammers. It was amazing to observe the construction crews enjoying music that may not be on their normal playlist. Through the entire construction and development process, a delightful, positive association existed among the crews, paying guests, musicians, and staff. Walking around the site with individuals or a quartet practicing was a healing and invigorating experience. After several years, the needs of the chamber music festival began to compete with an increased conference schedule and a demand for increased meeting space.

Construction began on the new Icicle Creek Music Center. It occupied the west twenty-five acres of the sixty-seven-acre Sleeping Lady site. By 2002 and 2003, those sixty-seven acres of Sleeping Lady were surveyed and legally divided into two separate sites and organizations. All the music center buildings were new construction, with the exception of Hermit Thrush. It was originally the manager's home at Camp Field and was moved to its present location west of the irrigation ditch. Hermit Thrush was gifted to the music center, and after extensive remodeling it became their office, with additional meeting and practice rooms.

Sleeping Lady received much publicity resulting from its association with Harriet but also through its emphasis on its own environmental sensitivity and natural setting. And Sleeping Lady has the good fortune to be within a two-hour driving distance from the major population center of Seattle. We learned many corporate meetings had an unofficial requirement of a maximum two-hour drive-time limit for multiday meetings or retreats away from the main office.

The University of Washington immediately became an important client of Sleeping Lady. Many government organizations found it difficult to use the conference site because of the cost involved. Word of mouth was an effective way to increase the use of the facility. Harriet made sure the food served was the best and used as much organic home grown produce as possible.

Two special meetings increased the positive reputation of Sleeping Lady: a Microsoft executive meeting and a North Atlantic Treaty Organization (NATO) Advanced Study Institute gathering.

Since Bill Gates would be in attendance, the director of Microsoft security made a trip to Sleeping Lady to check the effectiveness of providing security beforehand. The director shared with us their concern about meeting in Chelan County. Chelan County has had a reputation of having a very conservative population, with some indication of negative attitudes toward large corporations, especially those from western Washington.

The inspection passed with flying colors, but security guards were posted around the clock each day of the party's entire stay. There were many rumors in the local area about the nature of the Microsoft meeting at Sleeping Lady. One claimed the meeting involved a discussion about Microsoft purchasing the Seahawks football team.

At the end of the conference, several Microsoft employees visited each conference and sleeping rooms used by the party during their stay, collecting all papers left in waste receptacles or on tables to make sure no information was compromised. Microsoft paid to have exclusive use of the entire facility and grounds due to security considerations.

During August 1997, Sleeping Lady was the site of the Advanced

Study Institute of the NATO's two-week conference on sonochemistry and sonoluminescence. The conference included seventy-six leading scientists from around the world. Members were so appreciative of their stay that all seventy-six signed a thank you letter, with many adding delightful comments indicating their appreciation for the wonderful and productive conference experience. Dr. Larry Crum, of the applied physics lab at the University of Washington, headed this committee and conference. Dr. Crum went on to select Sleeping Lady for several other conferences and meetings.

In addition to numerous significant and exciting conferences, Harriet and her team also explored organizing gatherings or meetings that Sleeping Lady itself could initiate, providing additional paying business as well as promoting significant conversations to seek solutions to environmental and societal challenges.

In May 1997, Sleeping Lady organized and hosted the conference "On the Path to Simplicity." The concept of living simply was garnering a lot of attention in the early 1990s; many books were published on the subject. The first two people to become involved in the planning process were Cecil Andrews and Wenda O'Reilly. The others involved in the planning were John de Graaf, Duane Elgin, Vicki Robin, and Michael Schut. The other faculty members included Alan AtKisson, Ellen Furnari, Peter Hurley, John Schramm, and Wanda Urbanska. Forty-seven people registered for the conference representing nine states, including Vermont, Maryland, and Hawaii. One of the exciting features of the conference was the west coast premiere showing of the documentary *Affluenza—The Cost of High Living*. The documentary was directed and produced by John de Graaf.

In 1997, the Central Washington University alumni held a retreat at Sleeping Lady. During a conversation with a newly arrived faculty member, the idea of a film festival emerged. Mystery films were this faculty member's specialty, and this resulted in the Mystery Film Weekend at

Sleeping Lady, which started in 1997 and continued through 2004.

The weekend's program included three mystery films with specific themes or distinctive developments. Before each showing, information concerning the background of the film and its observable points were discussed. After each film, the group discussed the film and its individual impact. Mystery Film Weekend attracted thirty-five to forty people who were already registered at Sleeping Lady as well as those exclusively attending the Mystery Film retreat. Sleeping Lady's advantage in initiating these events was to allow scheduling during slower periods when the facility would likely have extra room.

The Hazel Wolf Film Festival began as the John de Graaf Film Festival. John was a successful documentary filmmaker and was associated with KCTS public broadcasting station in Seattle. The John de Graaf Film Festival was open to the public at no charge. It became clear, however, that if the film festival were to continue and expand. a more formal organization would need to organize and implement all the details.

Initially, Harriet provided direct and indirect subsidies to help launch the festival, but it would eventually need to carry its own costs. The film festival hired a part-time administrative assistant to direct the activities and assist with fundraising. The name of this new film festival was initially the Environmental Film Festival, then changed to the Equinox Film Festival, and its final name is the Hazel Wolf Film Festival. In April 2000, the film festival was dedicated to the memory of Hazel Wolf, a longtime environmental activist. Two of the keynote speakers for the festival included David Brower of the Sierra Club and Friends of the Earth, and Jennifer Belcher, member of the Washington State House of Representatives.

A number of documentary premieres occurred at the festival, and it also encouraged new documentary production. Two North Central Washington participants, Jamie Howell and Guy Evans, attended the festival in 2002 and were inspired to proceed with a documentary about the plight and future of orchards in North Central Washington. Their documentary was shown at a later Hazel Wolf Film Festival.

Another idea that was incorporated into the Sleeping Lady community was the Grotto Club. The idea of a lecture club had been discussed, and Harriet encouraged us to pursue this concept. It would involve a more intimate gathering of people who enjoy listening to and then discussing a wide variety of subjects. The implementation of the Grotto Club was another gift from Harriet, for she provided us with a great venue. Harriet thoroughly enjoyed the conversations and discussion. We invited presenters who would participate at no cost. Sometimes we provided a little wine, but most of the time it was like a potluck gathering, with many participants bringing treats. It took the name of the Grotto Club, because the initial gatherings were in the Grotto Bar at Sleeping Lady. Around thirty to thirty-five people could comfortably fit in the Grotto. Harriet's brother, Stimson Bullitt, was invited to be the inaugural speaker for the Grotto Club on November 23, 1996 with his presentation "Reflections on the Shape of Things to Come."

The Grotto Club did not have a specific schedule, but email invitations went out to those indicating an interest as speakers became available. The Grotto Bar was used for only a short time. As conference business increased, it was no longer available to the Grotto Club. So the club also met in O'Grady's Pantry, and for the final two years, Harriet suggested we use Coppernotch Lodge. Several of the presenters included Johnpaul Jones and Grant Jones, two of Sleeping Lady's principal architects; a photographer and poet; Bill Grace, director and founder of the Center for Ethical Leadership; Paul Roberts, author of the book *The End of Oil*, and Bill Jenkins, a favorite local resident who had worked within the complexities of the government for many years.

One of the final sessions of the Grotto Club was led by Erwin Janssen, MD, retired psychiatrist. He introduced the gathering to the concept of moral injury and its association with posttraumatic stress disorder, which many returning military personnel experience. Moral injury was also discussed concerning others outside of the military who have also experienced trauma in their lives.

The Coppernotch Lodge was the most enjoyable venue for the Grotto Club, and it was again made available through Harriet's generosity. Coppernotch was constructed in 1931, but unfortunately this beautiful structure was destroyed by a fire on September 12, 2014. It served the Bullitt family well for eighty-three years.

As the Sleeping Lady operation was improved and perfected, the Sleeping Lady Mountain Retreat became the Sleeping Lady Mountain Resort and took on a somewhat different operational style out of financial necessity. Conferences and meetings still provided a portion of the activity, but more emphasis was placed on individuals and families enjoying the matchless setting. Weddings were also promoted, becoming another lucrative portion of the business.

The Icicle Creek Music Center was expanded and renamed. The Icicle Creek Center for the Arts has an emphasis on the arts and theater as well as music.

During the years Harriet was developing the Sleeping Lady Mountain Retreat and the Icicle Creek Music Center, she was also involved in establishing other efforts to save the environment, preserving sensitive land and working to enhance the history and enjoyment of the Leavenworth community. Harriet established the Icicle Fund around 1998 as a 501(c)(3). Originally, the organization was focused on protecting the environment, advancing the arts, and promoting the natural and cultural history in the Wenatchee River watershed. The work quickly expanded to include the North Central Washington counties of Chelan, Okanogan, Douglas, and Grant.

Harriet selected Joan Alway as the first director of the Icicle Fund. Joan shared the following:

Harriet structured the Icicle Fund so that four of the Icicle Fund "partners" (The Nature Conservancy, Trust for Public Land, Chelan-Douglas Land Trust, and Audubon-Washington, which was later replaced by Barn Beach Trust) rotated through two voting seats annually. (Icicle Fund had a permanent voting seat). This meant these four partners had to get along, or as Harriet used to say, "had to play well together in the sandbox," since they would be voting on each other's proposals every other year. That was the structural aspect.

There was also an interpersonal one, in that all the board members who "got" Harriet's vision really bought into it and, I think, wanted to support and please Harriet. The question of "How could we work together on this?" was regularly posed. This tended to be most easily done among the environmental organizations, who excelled at it, but history and the arts were often in the mix.

I think the fact that Audubon was invited off the board was probably not lost on the participants. The same held for individual members who just wanted their share of the pie so they could go play in their own sandboxes, by themselves. These were not items that were really brought up or used as a warning, but they were part of the Fund's history.

Harriet was significant in jump-starting the great work of the Chelan-Douglas Land Trust. The trust was initially a totally volunteer organization. Bob Bugert, who served as the executive director of the trust for a number of years, shared that in the beginning, it became apparent the land trust could not achieve its goals on the shoulders of volunteers alone. The volunteers who had committed substantial resources to get the land trust in operation could not afford the type of investment needed to provide a full-time director to accomplish the real work needed to preserve land and habitat.

After considerable deliberation, the group agreed that this type of organization might appeal to Harriet Bullitt. Eliot Scull, the president of the organization at that time, agreed that he would reach out to Harriet to explain the situation—the goal of the land trust and the type of work their executive director would take on, as well as the long-term plan to sustain this position. With confidence, Eliot met with Harriet and respectfully asked her to contribute $5,000 to advance the work of the land trust. With a ready smile and an equally ready answer, Harriet countered with "Is that all you want?" and suggested $50,000. "If we are going to make this successful, let's do it right!" she asserted. How could Eliot disagree?

Since that initial gift, Harriet made several strategic investments into the land trust to allow it to achieve and broaden its goals. Bob indicated that all of Harriet's support has yielded tremendous results, but nothing was quite as endearing as that initial gift.

In 1999–2000, Barn Beach, a popular recreational area and swimming hole along the Wenatchee River close to downtown Leavenworth, was in jeopardy. Barn Beach was not only loved by locals but also had an emotional attachment for Harriet during her years growing up in the valley. Word spread quickly that a developer was purchasing the two and a half acres of land and planning a fifty-eight-unit condominium, which would cut off easy access to Barn Beach.

About the same time, Haus Lorelei on the River, a bed-and-breakfast operated by Elizabeth Saunders and her family, was up for sale. Harriet and the Icicle Fund purchased the building and property, initially giving it to the National Audubon Society. Eventually it became part of Barn Beach Reserve and later the Wenatchee River Institute. Barn Beach was saved, and a portion of Haus Lorelei became the home of the Upper Valley Museum.

Harriet became aware of a license for a FM radio station housed in

Leavenworth. The station was in a holding pattern and was just broadcasting recorded music twenty-four hours a day. Harriet's interest was in the license, which was owned by Jerry Isenhart, operating KOZI Radio in Chelan. Over time, and through extensive negotiations, Harriet not only purchased the license in Leavenworth but also purchased KOZI in Chelan.

Harriet wanted to establish a FM radio station in Leavenworth and was interested in using KOHO as the identification letters. She discovered KOHO was owned but not currently in operation, so she purchased the KOHO identification and established KOHO 101.1 FM. Originally, the station broadcast from the original Camp Field operation-registration office at the Sleeping Lady property entrance. Eventually the KOHO studio moved to Wenatchee, and the Sleeping Lady studio was remodeled into the existing Aspen Leaf Day Spa.

Harriet wanted to bring speakers and performers to Sleeping Lady that normally would be financially impossible, due to the limited amount of potential participants in the Wenatchee Valley. She worked with her attorneys to set up the Sleeping Lady Foundation, funded through Harriet, with the specific purpose of bringing special programs to the valley. There was a very reasonable charge for the events, with all proceeds donated to various local nonprofit organizations. These events were another of Harriet's gifts to the valley.

A brief list of significant speakers brought in by the Sleeping Lady Foundation through Harriet's generosity includes Temple Grandin, Morris Dees, Cesar Millan, Maya Lin, Luis Alberto Urrea, Zainab Salbi, and John Dau. At least one of the presentations required a single-night speaker's fee of $30,000, which illustrates the impossibility of bringing this caliber of speaker to a two-hundred-seat theater through local ticket sales alone. Harriet thoroughly enjoyed these presentations but also delighted in the fact that the valley could enjoy seeing and hearing these special guests in person locally.

Harriet loved the upper valley and did all she could to give the area opportunities to enjoy life at a new level. Her work to preserve nature continues to enhance the upper valley. Much of her work for preservation was behind the scenes, but it benefits not only the beauty of the area but also the businesses of the valley, who depend on the many visitors.

One of her long-term efforts was to again open Icicle Creek for migrating fish. Although she did not win all the battles she's initiated, she has been successful in helping groups in the area help maintain the purity of Icicle Creek to the greatest extent possible. The quality and variety of music has allowed many people of many backgrounds enjoy live music not normally available to a location with such a limited population.

To ensure the future operation of Sleeping Lady Mountain Resort and the continuation of the environmental work, the Icicle Fund was gifted the Sleeping Lady Mountain Resort operation, effective December 31, 2018.

Harriet is a special person in many ways. She is an athlete, an artist, an innovator, a developer, an equestrian student, and a protector of nature. But the one virtue that often is overlooked is her traditional gift of Christmas eggnog. Those employed by Harriet will never forget this special Christmas gift. I have personally, on several occasions, had the opportunity to enjoy this special treat.

The recipe didn't come from a bartenders' manual. The preparation of this delightful mix does not occur quickly. It is a mysterious operation. A wonderful history of the Bullitt eggnog actually appeared in an article by John Hinterberger in the *Seattle Times* on December 20, 1992.

The Bullitt eggnog tradition started with Harriet's mother Dorothy, who brought this liquid joy to her KING Broadcasting employees each Christmas. Harriet carried on the tradition during the early Sleeping

Lady years. The recipe actually goes back to 1912 and was brought to Seattle by Harriet's father, Scott, from Kentucky. According to oral history, the recipe was given to Scott by a musician and bartender at the Pendennis Club in Louisville. It has all the traditional ingredients (plus a few special items), but its secret is a forty-eight-hour "ripening," which is why most people won't give it a try. Harriet always insisted on using bourbon since the recipe originated in Kentucky. We can only hope that the recipe is stored in a safe place at Sleeping Lady and some associate has been carefully trained in its preparation. John's *Times* article had a wonderful description of the eggnog: "Ye gods and little fishes, this stuff is magic. Smooth as white racing silks, rich as Ross Perot, and just potent enough to cut through the richness with a keen and mellow alcoholic edge."

These conversations with Harriet and my personal experience in the development of Sleeping Lady Mountain Retreat and Icicle Creek Music Center share only some of the gifts Harriet has so graciously shared. Perhaps this writing will at least document a small portion of Harriet's life and provide a feel for her life's struggles, her delightful personality, and her boundless energy. I hope it will also provide a little insight into her generosity and love for the Leavenworth Valley. She valued friendship, and through friendship her generosity has been multiplied many times.

Many people have enjoyed the magical surroundings of Sleeping Lady, meeting to solve problems and initiate innovations. Artists have been discovered and encouraged. Musicians have been given inspiration and have trained to continue their journey toward perfection by sharing in a most unique setting. Volunteers, who individually have little power, have been invited to join together in organizations initiated and supported by Harriet, providing unbelievable results. Fish, in increasing numbers, are swimming up Icicle Creek. Helicopters that, forty years ago, made daily fights ferrying tourists up the Icicle Creek Canyon have not been seen or heard from the last thirty-nine years.

Harriet's feisty, loving nature may not have moved mountains, but it certainly kept the ones we have beautiful. Harriet has helped us understand that loving nature is a team sport.

Thank you, Harriet.

Made in the USA
Las Vegas, NV
12 July 2022